Dee Blick

Powerful Marketing
on a Shoestring Budget
For Small Businesses

authorHOUSE®

AuthorHouse™ UK Ltd.
500 Avebury Boulevard
Central Milton Keynes, MK9 2BE
www.authorhouse.co.uk
Phone: 08001974150

First published by AuthorHouse 12/8/2008

ISBN: 978-1-4389-3753-3 (sc)

Printed in the United States of America
Bloomington, Indiana

This book is printed on acid-free paper.

For Steven and Mark

Acknowledgements

Many people in my personal life have played a part in helping me to write this book. I am especially grateful to my lovely Mum for looking after the entire family whilst I was holed up in my office, my brother Andrew for his fantastic sense of humour and my husband Malcolm for being my biggest ally.

In my professional life, I am grateful to my small business clients for allowing me to share their stories of marketing success using these shoestring principles. I also want to give a big and heartfelt thank you to Gareth Sear of Walk and Travel, the inspiration and fount of knowledge behind Chapter 8.

Contents

Introduction

Marketing. It's a fascinating subject and one that I have devoted my entire career to. For many small businesses however, marketing is a black art, the preserve of big businesses with equally big marketing budgets.

Yet when harnessed properly, marketing is one of the most powerful and effective tools that a small business has at their disposal. If you want to grow and succeed in both good times and challenging times then you simply cannot afford to overlook the vital role that marketing plays in the long-term success of your business.

You don't need to be a marketing guru nor have a string of marketing qualifications to get some incredible results from your marketing efforts. The good news is that the best investment you can make where marketing your business is concerned is your time and enthusiasm. This doesn't mean that you have to spend four days a week on marketing, but if you can devote one day a month to focus on growing your business through marketing then you are off to an excellent start.

Marketing on a shoestring is all about combining your time and your energy with some marketing know-how and a splash of creativity. There's no need to spend huge sums of money on untested activities and then crossing your fingers in the hope that the results will justify the outlay. In fact, by following the advice in these pages you will find that your results go up and your marketing spend goes down!

And that's what this book is all about. No marketing jargon, just an abundance of accumulated wisdom, tips and some practical small business case studies that bring the advice to life. Whether you're just starting out, or have been in business for a few years, this book will help you understand how effective marketing activities can be performed on a small budget.

I hope you enjoy reading this book and that it inspires you to unleash the power and the potential of your small business.

Good luck!

Dee Blick

1 THE PRACTICAL SMALL-BUSINESS MARKETING PLAN

Before you consider spending money on marketing your business, it's essential to have a marketing plan in place. Sometimes, the thought of writing one conjures up visions of slaving away over a report that ends up at the bottom of a filing cabinet, never to be seen again! What is more many small-business owners believe that a marketing plan can only be written by marketing people, and don't see the point in having one without a healthy budget to back it up.

The good news is that creating a simple and effective marketing plan is within the grasp of *any* small business owner. Marketing qualifications are not necessary and nor is a big budget. A marketing plan is simply a practical document that can help a small business to grow by focusing on what they sell, who they should be selling to and ultimately, how they can achieve their sales targets. The cost of a marketing plan usually amounts to no more than your time. Even so, you don't have to set aside several days in your diary to write it. Chipping away at it for a few hours at a time should do the trick. There's no need to write long and elaborate paragraphs, a heading followed by a list of bullet points is just fine. A marketing plan is an action plan, not a thesis.

Once you have created your marketing plan, the real excitement begins as you start putting your ideas into practice. It's fair to say that over the years I have yet to encounter a small business that has not benefited from having a marketing plan no matter how simple or brief. However, I have met many small-business owners that have fallen into the common trap of spending huge sums of money on ineffective marketing, simply because they didn't have a marketing plan in place to guide them.

As you read through this chapter, you will learn how to create a marketing plan on a step-by-step basis. By way of illustration I will detail some small business case studies, describing the experience of working with a marketing plan. In particular, I will be describing the journey of one small business. Horsell Electrics are a family owned business specialising in making bespoke light fittings for a wide range of organisations including schools, airports, pharmaceutical companies and libraries. After spending thousands of pounds on marketing for very little return, the Managing Director decided to try again, but this time only after creating an all-important marketing plan. By reading this case study and those of other small businesses, I hope that the theory of marketing planning will be brought to life by actual experience.

In this chapter we are going to cover the following:

- Why bother with a marketing plan?
- Part One - Establishing realistic sales targets
- Part Two - Practical client research
- Part Three - What are your competitors doing and why should you care?
- Part Four - Reviewing and improving your overall offering
- Part Five - The price is right
- Part Six - Identifying your ideal clients
- Part Seven - Finding your ideal clients
- Are you ready to do business?
- Putting your marketing plan into practice

Why Bother with a Marketing Plan?

As mentioned earlier if you want results from your marketing without having to dig deep into your pockets, then a marketing plan is essential.

- o It helps provide clarity and direction. You take time out from the day-to-day running of your business to think strategically about how you want to grow it, where you want to take it.

- o It enables you to perform an audit of your business through a fact-finding process that encompasses your products and services, your people and your current and potential clients.

- o By establishing meaningful targets you are then able to focus on achieving them. The opposite is the case if you don't do this.

- o To quote Seneca, the Roman philosopher, "If one does not know to which port one is sailing, no wind is favourable."

Part One - Establishing Realistic Sales Targets

Staring at you is a blank piece of paper that is going to evolve into your marketing plan. What is the first thing that you should do, where do you begin? Start by thinking about where you want to take your business in the next 12 months through sales. With your marketing plan in place, you then work towards achieving these sales targets. You are probably in business because you are very good at what you do and you've identified a need. If you want your business to grow in both good times and challenging

3

times, then establishing realistic and measurable sales targets is important. They become the yardstick by which you measure your performance.

Many small businesses set unrealistic sales targets with little hope of achieving them. It's not unusual when watching business programmes to see small-business entrepreneurs making wild claims about their projected sales. The secret lies in establishing realistic sales objectives.
They need to be:

o   Measurable
o   Achievable
o   Time bound

Let's look at this in more detail.

Measurable and Achievable

Saying that you are hoping to "maximise your sales", or "massively increase your turnover" in the next year is neither specific nor helpful enough to give you an indication of where you are going. You need to establish hard targets that you can measure your performance against. Here are some examples of measurable sales targets.

o   In the next 12 months we aim to increase our sales from £48,000 to £60,000 through new clients.
o   In the next 12 months we aim to increase sales from existing clients from £150,000 to £175,000.
o   As a new business, in the next 12 months we aim to reach £35,000 of sales.

You can establish just one measurable sales target, but if you really want to channel your marketing activity in the right direction, you will benefit from taking a more detailed approach. Consider:

1. **Existing markets**
- how many sales are you planning to achieve from your existing markets with your existing products and services?

- how many sales are you planning to achieve from your existing markets with any new products and services?

2. **New markets**
- how many sales are you planning to achieve from brand new markets with your existing products and services?

- how many sales are you planning to achieve from brand new markets with any new products and services?

You may have no sales targets to put into No. 2 because you're not planning on venturing into any new markets in the foreseeable future. It could also be that you have no plans in the next year to introduce new products and services either. If this is the case, you will only have one sales target, which will fall into No.1. Continuing to sell your existing products and services to your existing markets carries much less risk than selling new products and services to new markets. It makes sense that if you are yet to take full advantage of opportunities offered within your existing markets selling your existing products and services, then moving into new markets is neither desirable nor necessary. However, only you know your business so think this through carefully before arriving at your sales targets.

Once you have made your decisions, it then comes down to ensuring that the figures staring back at you are achievable, even if attaining them is going to stretch you a little. Don't be tempted to pluck figures out of the air that appear impressive on paper but are in fact nothing more than flights of fancy.

Time bound

12 months is the time span you should establish in which to measure your performance against your sales targets. This allows sufficient time for your marketing activities to take effect and for you to measure progress.

Making any decisions based on a shorter timescale, or conversely allowing a marketing approach to continue beyond a year without review, could result in a productive activity being prematurely abandoned or an ineffective activity continuing for longer than necessary.

Part Two - Practical Client Research

You've completed the first part of your marketing plan and now it's time for some client research. It can be so easy when you are caught up in the day-to-day running of your business to overlook the importance of talking to your clients about what they really think of your products and services and the way that you communicate with them. But what has this client research got to do with your marketing plan? Actually, reaching your sales targets depends on you selling great products and services but you can only judge how good these are by asking the people that buy them what they think. So, client research is an important part of your marketing plan and it's easy to do.

Decide upon questions to ask.

Start by writing down the questions you would like to ask your clients. To help you, here are some possibilities:

- What influences you to buy from us?
- Where can we make improvements to our services and products?
- How can we make improvements to the way in which we deliver our services and products to you?
- How important is our price/fee structure in your decision to buy from us?
- If you had to give your top three reasons for doing business with us, what would they be?
- Do you also buy from any of our competitors?
- What are our competitors doing that you would like us to consider?
- What is your underlying need for our products/services? Do you anticipate this need changing in the next year?
- What do you think about our brand and our marketing communications?

Case Study: Horsell Electrics

Horsell Electrics wanted to find out from wholesalers and electrical contractors what they thought about their products and services and the Horsell brand. Rather than using a questionnaire they arranged an all-day event to celebrate their 60th anniversary. Over the course of the day they listened to their clients. The feedback was insightful and useful. Horsell Electrics were generally regarded as being more expensive than competitors for their standard range of products, but their made-to-measure light fittings in which they specialise were reasonably priced with no obvious competitors other than those based overseas. The Horsell brand itself was generally regarded as being old fashioned, with a lack of marketing activity being cited as the reason for this.

How can you find out what *your* clients think?

- **Pick up the telephone**, and ask if you can book a convenient time to gauge their feedback to your questions. This is probably the simplest approach available.

- **Invite a handful of clients to lunch.** It's a good idea to have someone with shorthand skills attend to take notes during the meeting. It will be impossible for you to talk and take notes at the same time. Be sure to brief your clients beforehand on the format of the event so there are no hidden surprises. You also need to clarify with each client that they are happy sharing feedback in a group rather than on a one-to-one basis.

- **Issue a simple questionnaire and follow up** with a telephone call. You won't get a huge number of responses using this approach but it is a low-cost method of obtaining very useful information.

Once you have gathered the feedback from your clients, it's time to return to your marketing plan. Summarise the key points that have been made by your clients and then make a note of the improvements you plan to make as a result of this feedback. Don't add these to your marketing plan just yet – you are going to address the whole area of improvement later on.

Part Three - What Are Your Competitors Doing and Why Should You Care?

You're now progressing your marketing plan nicely, having established some decent sales targets and engaged your clients with some timely market research. Competitor research is the next thing you need to turn your attention to. You've started the ball rolling by asking your existing clients if they use any of your competitors, but you need to go further. The good news is that you don't have to go overboard in researching your competitors and start producing complex tables etc. You can in fact spend too much time trying to discover what your competitors are up to and end up neglecting your own business. So let's consider exactly what information is going to be useful.

Identify your real competitors

How do you define a competitor to your business? It is easy to assume that competitors are everywhere, but you need to be very precise when evaluating other businesses as such.

If you are a local business working with clients in your local area, then a business doing the same thing many miles away is, in reality, unlikely to be a competitor. Even a business in your local area that is targeting local clients and offering similar services to you may not be a competitor if they are targeting a different *size* of client. You don't want to waste time researching businesses that do not turn out to be competitors after all.

How many competitors should you research? Aim for three or four. Any more and what should be a practical exercise becomes an academic one instead. Here are some useful things to learn about your main competitors:

o The name of their business and website
o Their products and services
o Their pricing strategy
o Their target audiences
o Their marketing literature
o How they promote themselves
o Their size and structure
o Where are they similar to you?
o Where are they better than you?
o What can you learn from their business?

The challenge now is gathering this information. This should be a relatively easy exercise.

- **Google the name of each competitor** and it should yield information that ranges from a few paragraphs to several pages. In my experience this is one of the most effective ways to find out as much as you can about your competitors.

- **Visit their website.** Company websites are very useful for sharing information. Make sure that you read the news page if there is one as this often includes recent client signings and news about their business progress in general.

- **Ask friends and relatives** if they don't mind posing as mystery shoppers. You need to bear in mind that if you ask them to gather too much detailed information, they will probably arouse suspicion.

- **Ask your business colleagues and fellow networkers** if they have any knowledge about your competitors that they would be willing to share with you.

Follow these steps and you will be in a position whereby you have answered most, if not all, of the questions on your list and now have a great deal of useful information and knowledge. Allocate one page of your marketing plan to each competitor. Detail each question and include the information you have gathered underneath in bullet points. You are going to be referring back to this valuable information as you progress through your marketing plan.

Part Four - Reviewing and Improving Your Overall Offering

A client does not base the decision to buy from you purely on the strengths of your product. There are a number of other factors that affect this decision, including:

- o Your reputation
- o Your delivery terms
- o Your flexibility and availability
- o Your payment terms
- o The personal service given by everyone in the team

How you sell and how you subsequently look after your clients is just as important as the product or service itself. Your marketing plan is the ideal place in which to scrutinise your service as a whole. You have already started this by asking your existing clients how they view the experience of working with you and have looked at how you compare with your competitors. The information gathered in these exercises should enable you to identify the areas in which improvements can be made. Bring these findings into your marketing plan. Whether you are a small home-based business or have a team of people working alongside you, don't ignore the value that is to be gained from improving what you offer. Your marketing plan is the perfect vehicle to help you make this happen. Here's how:

- **Analyse the information that you have gathered** through your competitor and client research. What lessons can be learned? Are there improvements that need to be made to match the offerings from your competitors? Has your client feedback highlighted an area in which you could provide additional value? Review your products and services. Identify any changes that can be made immediately and any that perhaps require more time or money before being implemented. List all these improvements in your marketing plan.

- **Imagine now that you are in a perfect business** world where neither budget nor resources are lacking and you can make any number of positive changes to your products and services. What changes would you make? Draw up a list and put these in your marketing plan under the heading of 'ambitious changes'. You may not be in a position to make them now or in the foreseeable future but when you don't limit your thinking with everyday business worries or challenges, you can often come up with the most amazing ideas. It is easy to dismiss great ideas simply because you don't currently have the resources to implement them. From now on retain these ideas and add them to your marketing plan. It's possible that at some stage you will implement some of these ideas and they could make a dramatic improvement to your business.

- **Look at things slightly differently.** So far you have been considering how to improve or increase what you offer, however reducing your offering may be just as powerful. If you offer a product or a service for which there appears to be little demand and this lack of interest seems likely to continue in the future, you need to consider removing it. This situation arose with an IT maintenance business that sold a range of computer hardware in addition to their main business services. Despite investing thousands of pounds promoting computer hardware to their existing clients and cold prospects, there was little demand. In fact when reviewing their products and services as part of building their marketing plan they discovered that it was costing them more to market these products than they were gaining in sales. They immediately stopped selling computer hardware and focused solely on the profitable part of their business. In hindsight this decision should have been made many months earlier, but it was only through the process of standing back from the business and reviewing it as part of their marketing plan that they discovered the full extent of the problem.

Earlier, we noted the fact that clients buy more from you than just your products and services, so it's important to consider how you can improve the overall experience. Start by identifying three changes that you can make that will have an immediate positive effect. Consider also any improvements that you can make in the longer term. What would these improvements look like if you had no restrictions whatsoever? Using the same approach outlined earlier, go back to your marketing plan and make a small list of the improvements that you can implement now, the improvements you can make in the next 12 months, and finally the improvements that you would make if you had unlimited time and money. Here are some examples of immediate improvements that small businesses can make:

o Introducing a personal call handling service. Rather than being put through to a voicemail when the phone is engaged, clients are greeted by a friendly and professional person instead.

o Reducing the response time to client e-mails
o Reducing the turnaround time on orders
o Reducing the time spent on back-office paperwork, shifting the focus back to communicating more frequently with your clients
o Adding a personal note of thanks to accompany orders
o Following up on every client session with a positive e-mail

Case Study: Horsell Electrics

The review process was an exciting part of the marketing plan for Horsell Electrics and it led to significant improvements in the business. Clients were more than happy with the bespoke products offered and the positive feedback included the fact that complex light fittings could be made from very basic drawings. Because the business was UK-based, clients felt that any problems were resolved quickly, whereas the opposite was the case with manufacturers based overseas. However, many clients also commented that they would like Horsell to deliver a faster turnaround on these bespoke products in order to meet the tight deadlines imposed by their own clients. As a result of this feedback the business embarked on an internal improvement programme called 'Lean Manufacturing', with the Manufacturing Advisory Service. Every single process in the manufacturing plant was analysed and improved. This had the intended effect of improving their overall turnaround times.

Case Study: Mantra Magazines

The team at Mantra Magazines produce two local magazines in West Sussex, RH10 Uncovered and RH19 Uncovered. As part of their review and improvement process they invited readers to give feedback on what they liked about the magazines and where improvements could be made. The positive feedback was that each magazine included topical articles, interesting local features and relevant community news. Because the businesses advertising in the magazines were local too, readers felt that the advertising element was relevant and useful. However, some readers made the suggestion that the magazines could be improved by including content relevant to home-based businesses, given that this applied to a significant proportion of the readership. This led to a brand new business section called 'The Biz-to-Biz Hub' where guest writers were invited to write useful business tips and articles for the small business run from home. The knock-on effect of this new section was that advertising revenues increased due to additional interest from businesses wanting to market their products and services to the home-based businesses market.

Part Five - The Price Is Right

Your marketing plan should also define your pricing strategy. You need to understand how your prices differ from those of your competitors and so determine your general approach to pricing. You can't establish pricing in isolation based purely on what you would like to charge.

In order to ascertain your pricing strategy there are two boundaries to observe. The lower boundary is the cost of your products or services; the upper boundary is the price charged by your dearest comparable competitor. It goes without saying that if you are selling at cost or less, you're unlikely to be in business very long. If you're selling at the highest boundary, the same situation could apply unless you are able to demonstrate that your product or service exceeds anything that your nearest competitor is offering. Even then, clients have to be willing to pay more for the added value.

With your marketing plan, you are able to stand away from your business and evaluate your approach to pricing, looking at where and how you add value. After researching your competitors and speaking with your clients, it is likely that you now have a clearer understanding of the impact that your prices have on your clients' decisions to buy.

Write this down. You don't need to go beyond a paragraph but you do need to consider these factors before arriving at your price strategy.

Case Study: Specialist Recruitment Consultancy

This is a small business that specialises in the recruitment of care staff from overseas that are then placed in UK based care homes. The price strategy of this business is to charge fees that are higher than most of their competitors. They do this because they have sufficient clients willing to pay more for what they believe is a benefit that no one else offers. This benefit is that if a care worker that has been placed by the recruitment consultancy leaves within 12 months, they are replaced at no additional cost to the client. This compares favourably with their nearest competitors who offer only a three-month or six-month replacement guarantee. The recruitment consultancy can therefore charge more because they have created real value for their clients - value that clients recognise and are willing to pay for.

Case Study: Horsell Electrics

As outlined earlier, the research Horsell Electrics undertook with their clients was important in defining their pricing strategy. By electrical wholesalers, they were regarded as being more expensive than other suppliers for standard fittings, but their made-to-measure light fittings were regarded as being reasonably priced. This feedback had a real impact on how Horsell Electrics began to market their products. Their emphasis changed from trying to market their standard products to focusing instead on their made-to-measure light fittings.

They identified the products in their standard range where they were able to match competitor prices and promoted these to wholesalers by using incentives to encourage a switch. This approach proved to be very successful. Requests for quotations from wholesalers increased for both the standard light fittings being promoted and the made-to-measure light fittings. Horsell Electrics also began to target a group of potential clients known as 'specifiers' (clients such as architects that specify the supplier they want a tradesman to use when working on one of their projects). Research had revealed that specifiers were usually more concerned about the quality of a product and working with a local accountable supplier, than they were with haggling for the lowest price.

Part Six - Identifying Your Ideal Clients

You are making real progress now! You've established your sales targets, done some practical client and competitor research, identified some improvements to your products and services and you're now clear about your pricing strategy and where you deliver value. There's one big piece of the jigsaw still missing...

Who are you going to sell to?

When I ask a small-business owner this question the response tends to be "everyone needs our services." This may be true, but attempting to target everyone is not the right way to go about getting business. There will be some groups that have a much greater need for your products or services than others. The secret lies in *finding* them rather than communicating to all and sundry. There are strong benefits to this targeted approach.

- **As a small business, you don't have unlimited** time to spend on marketing. By targeting your ideal prospective clients, you focus your time and enthusiasm on the groups that have a deep underlying need for your products or services (and where you know that you can deliver to a high standard). It's the dream of most small business owners - building high-value relationships with clients that love their products and services.

- **You will grow.** Adopting a targeted approach to finding new clients as opposed to a more random approach gets you on to the fast track to business growth. Your marketing messages are powerful and focused because you understand what triggers your target audience to buy.

How can you find your ideal Clients?

Start by defining your ideal client. Some characteristics that define them may include:

- o They pay on time
- o They have a genuine need for what you offer
- o They make the decision to do business with you in a short space of time
- o They recommend you to other ideal clients
- o They are happy with your prices
- o They are easy to identify and communicate with

What else do you want to add to this list? Return to your marketing plan and make a list of the attributes of your ideal client. It is simple enough to do and yet it focuses you on attracting the people that you want to do business with and in turn helps you to rule out others that are less suitable. For example, you will not necessarily want to attract people that try to barter down your prices to the point where you're not making any money.

It's time now to ask another question, "Are my ideal clients all the same or do they fall into different groups?" It's unlikely that your ideal clients will all fall into one group. The common thread that binds them is the need they have for your products or services. What sets them apart is how they express that need. You can see this illustrated in the following example of a personal fitness instructor that identified three groups of ideal clients for his business:

o Individual clients that work with him on a one-to-one basis to improve their personal fitness. Whilst they share a common need to get fit, they have different reasons for doing so, from training for a marathon to losing weight and toning up.

o Local businesses that ask him to run sessions on their premises aimed at benefiting their staff. What unites these different businesses is that they recognise their obligation as responsible employers to promote the well-being of their employees in the workplace. Although each business varies, most of their employees spend their working day at a desk using a computer.

o Weight loss instructors and slimming consultants that pay him to deliver motivational talks to members on the benefits of getting fit and toned as a way of helping to lose weight.

By identifying only those groups that have the greatest need for his services, he can deliver targeted messages that are both attractive and specific to each group. The message to a local business looking for fitness sessions for desk-based employees would differ from the message to a weight loss instructor. Whilst he could say with accuracy that everyone has a need for his services, not everyone will recognise or express that need. He wants to focus his energies on targeting those groups of potential clients that recognise the benefits of using him and that want to do so in the immediate future.

Using this example to guide you, start by making a list of the different groups that you would like to target. Don't forget to include your existing clients. If you are looking for repeat business from clients in the next 12 months, they will be one of your targeted groups. Once you've got your list, whittle it down to a handful that you would really like to target in the next 12 months. These are the groups which

o You believe they have a deep need for your products or services.
o You are confident that you can deliver to a high standard.
o You believe they will buy from you in sufficient quantities (so enabling you to reach your sales targets).
o You are confident of reaching sufficient numbers within that group.

Once you have finalised your list add it to your marketing plan, making sure to leave space to add some more information as it's time now to build a detailed understanding of each group. Let's use the example of a bookkeeper to illustrate this. She is planning to introduce her bookkeeping services to accountants, but how can she progress from defining the sector of accountants, to identifying only those accountants with whom she wants to do business? Well, she may only want to target accountants that

o Are based in her local district.
o Only work with small businesses.
o Are small practices of just one qualified accountant with no support staff.

By drilling down to the types of accountants she wants to work with, she is eliminating thousands of others that she does not need to target.

If you can spend some time building up a detailed picture of each one of your target markets, you're going to be in a position where you will focus your energies on communicating with your hottest prospects, rather than communicating with huge numbers of which many may be unsuitable targets. When you have finished this, go back to your marketing plan. This is going to be your working document so it's important that you include all this useful information in it.

But you're not quite finished yet with your ideal targeted clients. It is time now to find them.

Part Seven - Finding Your Ideal Clients

Your marketing plan is gathering pace. You're not thinking of targeting everyone with your products and services, opting instead for the less is more approach. The challenge now lies in locating your groups of targeted clients. It's not that difficult and can begin with some brainstorming ... followed by more lists!

Case Study: Horsell Electrics

Architects were identified as one important sector that Horsell Electrics wanted to target. This was because architects usually specify the lighting manufacturer that they want an electrical contractor to use. Within the sector of architects, the following criteria was established to identify the most suitable ones to target:

o *Architects based in the East Sussex area*

o *Architects that specialise in commercial projects and projects for schools, councils and libraries etc*

Finding them proved to be easy and didn't cost anything. A search on the Internet revealed www.architecture.com, the official website of the Royal Institute of British Architects (RIBA). It was possible to search for members using the simple criteria specified above. Several influential local architects were targeted by mail, then contacted by telephone and invited to lunch. Their feedback from what proved to be the first of many events was invaluable in shaping the marketing activities that followed. Richard Ainsworth, the Managing Director, established a 12 month networking programme aimed at architects and other specifiers and launched a gallery showcasing young innovative lighting designers and celebrating the beauty within British manufacturing. All this was achieved on a small budget. A room that had previously been used for stock was emptied and transformed into a gallery. The Manufacturing Advisory Service became sponsors for the gallery, which provided a financial shot in the arm as well as giving kudos to the project. Horsell Electrics are now being asked to provide quotations by architects and other specifiers that prior to this marketing activity would not have considered the Business. Previously, the Horsell brand was seen to be old-fashioned; this is now no longer the case.

Here are some suggestions to help you find your targeted clients:

- **Search on the Internet**. It's likely that you will find websites, forums and discussion groups from which you can locate your target groups and build your contact lists.

- **If you are a member of your local Chamber of Commerce**, ask if they can direct you to the information you are looking for. Also, your local Business Link is a great place to ask about the free help and guidance available (*www. businesslink.gov.uk*).

- **Is there a membership organisation that represents** any of your targeted groups, as with RIBA for architects? They may furnish you with the information you are looking for and may even allow you to make offers to their members. Do they have events or meetings that you can attend?

- **Are there any local or national networking groups** that are aimed at your targeted groups? For example, one small business wanted to target local businesses within the construction sector. He discovered a construction specific networking group only a few yards from the offices where he worked and obtained many clients from attending this group.

- **Business directories, telephone directories,** local business magazines, newspapers, community directories and online directories can all be incredibly useful for sourcing information. For example, the personal fitness instructor mentioned earlier found his business clients from a local business directory and from searching on the Internet for slimming groups.

- **If you belong to a networking group** why not ask the members if they can help you? Within the group there are probably a few businesses that fall into your category of ideal clients, so find out from them where you can also target their peers.

- **If you're not a member of your local library**, then now is the time to join. Libraries are really useful places for tracking down information on your target audiences also.

This is a task that you don't have to complete all in one go. In fact spending 10 or 15 minutes here and there and making notes when you discover a real gem is more than good enough. You don't need to spend hours on end looking for inspiration. Keep adding to your list every time you think of something new or receive a recommendation. You will end up with a well-researched, practical and useful list enabling you to spring into action. Make sure that this list is added to your marketing plan.

But before we look at how you're going to target your ideal clients, there is one thing left to do. You need to review your business and identify any changes that need to be made in order to accommodate the sales when they start rolling in.

Are you Ready to do Business?

As discussed throughout this chapter, the idea behind your marketing plan is to achieve your sales targets by focusing your energies on the potential and existing clients that really want your products and services.

As part of this process, you also need to ensure that your business is completely aligned with achieving your goals. When the new business starts flowing as your marketing plan is put into practice, you need to be in a position to cope without any major problems or challenges. Explaining to clients that the reason they are experiencing problems is down to issues with your system or your staff due to increased activity won't wash. You need to look at

- o Your operational capabilities.
- o Your resources.
- o The culture of your organisation.

Let me illustrate this with another example. A small business owner made the decision to franchise her successful business. She was so successful in recruiting franchisees that within 10 months she had reached her two-year franchisee target. The problem was that although she had developed a superb marketing and training programme for her franchisees, she had not considered the impact that these extra people would have on her operational capabilities and resources. Whereas the existing administration system had been more than adequate for her business, it proved to be less than capable in supporting the demands of the 12 franchisees that were now placing orders and making enquiries on a daily basis. Her human resources were stretched to the limit too. The team found it virtually impossible to deliver their usual high standards of service to the franchisees and a string of complaints led to many becoming de-motivated and unhappy. This placed a strain on the business owner too. She had to move away from generating new business and supporting her franchisees to fire fighting and processing orders. The situation was eventually rectified with a new and improved administration system, new team members and regular team meetings. However, it goes without saying that it would have been much better for everyone involved if a proper assessment of the business had been made before the marketing plan was put into action.

Now this may be a fairly dramatic example but it does illustrate the importance of considering the impact that a significant increase in new business could have on your business. There may be no need to make any changes, or it could be that you just need to tweak a few things. But by addressing the areas where you think change may be in order, you can put your marketing plan into action confident that you can handle the new business that is going to come your way. With Horsell Electrics most of the change centred on the manufacturing plant after the introduction of the Lean Manufacturing programme. With other small-business clients change has been minimal but nevertheless, it has been needed.

One business owner recruited a part-time administrator to handle the additional paperwork generated by the increased sales activity. Another brought in a commission only sales person to handle the new leads that arose from the marketing activity.

If you want to implement your marketing plan without hitting any major stumbling blocks, be aware of the possible need to make changes to accommodate the new business.

Putting Your Marketing Plan into Practice

The time has come to roll out your marketing plan with some simple but powerful marketing tactics. The chapters that follow show how to achieve your sales targets on a small budget. Before racing ahead, though, here are some tips that will help you put your plan into practice.

- **Plan your marketing activity in three-month segments.** If you're embarking on your marketing programme at the beginning of January, plan your activities from January to the end of March. Three months is a manageable period for most small businesses to work with, and it allows sufficient time to understand what is working and what is not.

- **When considering which marketing tactics to use,** always refer back to your marketing plan where you identified the different groups you want to reach and where to find them. This should influence your choice of marketing tools. For example, if the only way that you can reach a group is through renting or buying a mailing list, it's likely that targeted direct mail and the telephone will be your marketing tools of choice.

- **Although it is tempting to focus on one marketing tactic** because you like the sound of it, for example business networking, it's always a good idea to consider three or four different tactics to help you reach your key target audiences. Don't put all your eggs in one basket unless you are confident that one marketing tactic on its own is going to deliver results. The advantage of selecting a handful of tactics is that you can 'blend' your activities together to increase responses. For example, if you follow up leads gained from exhibiting with a telephone call, you will receive more positive responses than if you rely upon those people to contact you. Bear in mind that the target audiences you have identified will usually need more than one communication before making the decision to do business with you. It takes time to build up trust, whether that amounts to days, weeks or months. Look at how you can blend your marketing tactics for maximum impact.

Before you commit to spending *any* money on *any* marketing activity, ask yourself the following questions.

- o Will I reach my target clients and if so, do I know how many?
- o Will this enable me to communicate the benefits of doing business with me to my target audience?
- o What are the three key business benefits of selecting this activity?
- o How can I blend this to increase its impact?
- o How much is it going to cost me?
- o What return do I need to achieve to make it worthwhile?

By running through these questions, you will establish whether the marketing activity you are looking at represents a wise investment or is a waste of time and money.

Commit to marketing and you will be rewarded

The businesses that are successful at marketing on a shoestring are the ones that commit their time and energy on an ongoing basis. When business is going very well, they still carry on with their marketing. When business is sluggish, they redouble their marketing efforts. They don't stop and start their marketing activity. They put marketing at the centre of everything they do and in doing so, are rewarded with success. As you read through these chapters, I hope that you are inspired with ideas to grow your business through marketing and that you achieve some fantastic results through doing so.

2 THE SECRETS OF SUCCESSFUL NETWORKERS

The benefits of business networking were driven home to me when I started my business with nothing other than a robust marketing plan, a small loan from my Dad and bags of determination to succeed. I joined a local business networking group that entailed getting up at the crack of dawn once a week and heading off to a nearby hotel, armed with business cards, a one-minute presentation and any props that would make my presentation memorable. Within just two months of joining, I had enough new business from this group to keep me very busy for the next six months. The benefits did not stop there. I made some great business contacts, found reliable and talented new suppliers and was able to bounce ideas off a group of like-minded but diverse business people.

I am still a member of this networking group and I also attend several networking events each month, ranging from informal business networking in the evening over a curry to one-off local events with guest speakers and some lively debate to spice things up.

Success through business networking is within the grasp of any small business. Thousands of small businesses week in week out are transforming their bottom line through networking regardless of what they do for a living. Whether you're a plumber or a web developer, networking can work for your business providing you are willing to give it your very best shot.

Like all marketing tools though, for business networking to really deliver a return you have to be prepared to invest your time and energy, to learn some new skills and to polish up existing ones.

What's remarkable about business networking is that it ticks all the boxes of the marketing on a shoestring philosophy. Compare the cost of networking with other marketing activities and it comes up trumps every time. With nothing more than a decent line of conversation and some business cards to hand out, you can get incredible results. This isn't just my experience, it's the experience of the many businesses that I have worked with over the years and the many more that I have met at networking events. All would heartily endorse networking as a fundamental method for generating new business. In this chapter, we're going to cover the following:

- What is business networking?
- The benefits of networking to a small business
- The natural fears about business networking
- The importance of research
- Attending networking events
- How to benefit from online business networking
- The common types of networker
- How to be remembered for all the right reasons
- Your one-minute chance to shine
- Measuring the impact of your networking

Throughout this chapter I will introduce you to 12 business people. Each one runs a successful small business. They are a diverse group, but what unites them is that they are all successful at growing their businesses through business networking. In their own words, they will share with you their personal secrets for business networking success. I am sure that they will inspire you.

What Is Business Networking?

Business networking is no more than the process of establishing mutually beneficial relationships with other business people and potential clients. It encompasses the way in which you relate to the people and resources around you.

The words 'mutually beneficial' are so important - business networking is not about trying to hard sell and coerce people into doing business with you. It is about establishing links and partnerships that benefit everyone involved. It works on the simple principle of word-of-mouth recommendation. If you are good at what you do and people know about this, then you will be recommended.

"Being natural is key and that means being yourself! I don't have an opening pitch as every situation and person is different. Often the opening is as simple as "Hello, I am Eve.... what is your line of business?" Asking open questions gets the conversation flowing and gives me the opportunity to talk about my business later on with the advantage that I can tailor what I do to their needs because I know a little more about them. I also like to help people and if I can do this with contacts and information then I will. I firmly believe that your positive approach and friendliness will pay you back in kind."

Eve Clennell, Managing Director Eden HR Consulting

"I believe you have to be honest and sincere and if you approach networking with a view that all you want to do is get business for your own business, you will ultimately be found out. Aim to build strong and positive relationships with people and don't be in it just for yourself! Work hard at finding business for the people that you network with at the same time as looking and listening for an opportunity to sell your own services."

Mike Potts, Director Flightstore

The Benefits of Networking to a Small Business

There are so many benefits that we could fill the entire chapter discussing them. These, however, are seven key benefits:

o   You can develop profitable long-term relationships with the people you are networking with, relationships that lead to new clients and new sales for your business.

o   You can share and exchange useful and interesting ideas. In this way you benefit from the experience of others without having to pay for it.

o   Your new business acquisition costs are low because you do not have to pay for good leads beyond your networking fees.

o   If you're willing to share your ideas and your knowledge, then in no time you can become an opinion leader, a person that other people look up to and seek out. This has many PR advantages.

o   Knowledge is power and networking with different people from a wide range of sectors and businesses really helps to build your commercial knowledge.

o   Your presentation skills and confidence improve in leaps and bounds. Networking offers many opportunities for you to develop new skills including public speaking and face-to-face client presentations.

o   By joining a networking organisation that requires regular attendance, you immediately find yourself with a brand new sales force and without the need to pay commission or salaries for the privilege. Your fellow members are on the lookout for new business opportunities for you as they go about their daily work.

Like all good marketing ideas, the networking concept is a very simple one. The more people with whom you can build a good relationship, that really understand what you do and the target markets that you want to reach, the larger your pool of good quality leads will be. The message is clear – networking works, but you have to work at it if you want results.

"I'm a firm believer that networking is an effective and positive way to develop your business. Networking has helped me build a very strong client base and it's a gateway to building relationships with suppliers and key business people that have offered me invaluable support in many ways. My tips for networking are; be consistent, listen and show interest in other people and always be enthusiastic about the benefits you offer rather than who you are."

Allison Golding, Publisher and Editor Business Talk Magazine

The Natural Fears About Business Networking

Take a look at the list of common networking fears below and the chances are that you'll identify with some, if not all of them. I have certainly suffered from all of them at one time or another.

- o They might not like me

- o What if I get there and I'm the last person to enter the room?

- o What if I get there and I'm the first person to enter the room?

o   What if I run out of things to say?

o   What if I am left standing on my own?

o   What if I sound breathless when I start speaking?

o   Why on earth am I here?

o   I get nervous at the thought of public speaking

o   I am no good at making small talk

o   What if I get stuck with someone that I don't like?

Few of the confident and successful networkers that you meet were born that way. They started networking with these fears and they worked through them. Once you really get in to the swing of networking on a regular basis, you will find that most of these fears will disappear through a combination of familiarity, practice and polish.

The Importance of Research

Joining a business networking group

The biggest investment that you make when you add networking to your list of marketing activities is undoubtedly your time and your commitment. Unlike advertising, where you can part with a sizeable sum of money but the advert then does the work for you, with networking you spend a small sum of money and do all of the legwork. That said, it is usually both enjoyable and rewarding.

However, you don't want to invest your time in a networking group that turns out to be unsuitable for a variety of reasons. It's important that you do some practical research beforehand. Here are some tips to help you find the right networking group:

- **Draw up a shortlist of all the networking groups** that are in the geographic area that you cover. If you don't know where to start, ask your local Chamber of Commerce or Business Link for a list of networking organisations in the area. Use the Internet, go along to your local library and ask other business people if they belong to a group. Business Networking International (*www.bni.co.uk*), the networking group to which I belong, is the largest business-networking organisation in the world. It is more than likely that there will be at least one if not several BNI networking groups in your area in addition to other networking groups that meet regularly.

- **Find out if the Federation of Small Businesses** (*www. fsb.org.uk*) organises networking events in your area. Your local FSB branch may run evening and morning networking events for members and non-members alike. I am a member of the FSB and joined for the networking benefits and for the fact that the FSB lobbies government on behalf of small businesses. Their membership package is extremely good and the joining fee is very reasonable. Well worth looking into.

- **At the end of this research** you will have a list of different networking groups and their contact details. It's a good idea to find out as much as you can on each group before you start to do your rounds of those that, on the face of it, tick all of your boxes. Make sure that you get the answers to the following questions:

  o How many members belong to the group? If you are looking to join a networking group to get new business rather than just to socialise and make new business contacts, then it's a good idea to join a group that has a decent number of members, ideally 15 or more. The more members there are, the more chance there is of you getting warm leads.

o What kinds of businesses have joined? Look for businesses you can forge common links with. For example, a financial adviser would share common ground with an accountant, as would a marketing person with a graphic designer. Look at the profile of each member and ask yourself how many of them will be in a position to recommend potential clients to your business. Then turn the tables around. Are you going to be able to recommend prospects and clients to them? If you want to win friends and influence people, then you're going to have to give as well as gain.

o How is the group structured? Is there a membership committee or does the group rely upon the goodwill of individual members to keep it going? Groups that have an established membership committee with clearly defined roles tend to be better organised and more focused than those that rely upon ad-hoc gestures of help.

o When do you attend? Some networking groups require a weekly attendance where you usually network over breakfast. Other groups meet on a monthly basis, either over lunch or in the evening. Whilst it is true that few people welcome the prospect of an early start, there are some advantages from attending an early morning group. Once there, you're alert and ready to do business. You can even be back at your desk by 09:00am!

    o Can anyone join the group even if there is an existing member in the same profession? The more successful networking organisations only allow one member from each profession to join their group. This means that once you've signed on the dotted line and paid your membership fee, you're not going to be looking over the breakfast table at one of your competitors. Additionally, if a competitor is already a member then the reputation that they will have already built up with the members will make it harder for you to get recommendations and sales.

    o What are the costs? At this stage, it's useful to know if there are any joining fees, annual membership fees and fees to cover your regular attendance. Make sure that you also include any parking costs and other miscellaneous expenses associated with your networking.

Once you've done your homework on the networking organisations in your area, it's time to pay a visit to the ones that have really sparked your interest. To be allowed to visit, you usually only need to pay a small fee to cover your attendance and any refreshments. You never know if you ask nicely you may even get invited for free!

"For me, effective business networking is ultimately about building people relationships. So, be curious. Ask great questions and listen. When we listen and stop planning what to say next, we have good conversations and we start to build better relationships. Focus on being abundant. Give advice, help and support whenever you can, particularly in your areas of expertise. In my experience, having people talking about your abundance is at the centre of building raving fans. It's also really important to follow up on conversations you've had when networking. Don't say, "I'll call you" unless you intend to do so

promptly. Fulfilling every commitment shows that you are credible and reliable. Finally, have fun and be upbeat!"

Keith Roberts MBA, Certified Action Business Coach

Time now to use your eyes, ears and intuition

So, you've made it through the door. Good. But rather than just being a passive spectator, make sure that you really focus on finding out whether this group is going to benefit your business and whether you can be of benefit to the existing members. Here are some things to consider when judging the group:

- **What kind of welcome do you receive from the members?** If it is natural and friendly and you get plenty of smiles and interest, then you are off to a very good start.

- **What is the general atmosphere within the room?** Is it positive, professional and welcoming or does it feel like a closed shop where the members have become so friendly with one another that visitors are overlooked? Is there a buzz in the air with lots of animated conversations or is it a bit flat and humourless?

- **What are the members like?** Ultimately, people buy from people and it's important that you form a positive impression about the people that are in that room. If you join, you will be meeting these people week in week out and in all likelihood recommending them to your contacts as well as expecting recommendations back.

- **How is the meeting structured?** Is it interesting and positive? Is there a programme of speakers and presentations or is it a more informal discussion group? Is it a blend of both? Does it start later than billed? Does it overrun or is it well organised and on time?

- **What are your membership obligations?** It's always worth asking the existing members this question. Before you sign up to any organisation, you need to find out what happens if you are unable to attend due to either work or holiday commitments. Do you have to find someone to take your place on these occasions? At some stage will you be expected to join the membership committee? Again, don't be put off by membership obligations. A well-run group that is focused on generating business for members will tend to have rules and regulations that are designed to benefit everyone.

- **What quality of recommendations** (often known as referrals) are the members passing to one another and in what quantities? You will find on your travels that the number of referrals that are passed by the members in each group varies. In the networking group that I belong to, where we have 40 members, we manage to pass around 50 referrals every week. This is very high. At the other end of the scale, I have visited many different networking groups where only five referrals have been passed between 15 members. Listen intently to the type of recommendations that are being handed out. Are they good quality, warmed up leads or just telephone numbers plucked from a phone book? Really pay attention to this part of the meeting so that you can get a feel for how much effort each member is putting into the referrals they are giving.

- **Not all networking groups actively pass referrals** to one another on an organised basis. Many networking groups adopt a far more informal approach where members simply network and discuss business before enjoying the refreshments and listening to the speakers that follow. Alternatively, they can simply comprise of a group of business people that get together to share ideas and help one another out. There is no emphasis on generating business for one another. At the end of the day it comes down to you deciding on the format and structure that you prefer. You can only do this if you have visited several networking organisations and compared differing structures, objectives and membership profiles. However, if you are looking to gain new business from networking, then joining a group that is focused on passing business rather than just having a good time is the best place to start.

To join or not to join? That is your next question.

By now, you should have a good idea of the group that you would like to join. However, it's always worth going back a second or third time before signing on the dotted line. This is especially important if your first and only visit to a group has been on a day where each member is encouraged to bring a visitor. Go back after visitors' day so you can see exactly how many members belong to the group. I attended one networking group where over 60 businesses were present because it was an organised visitors' day. Although tempted to join I went back on a normal day and only 14 members were present.

Look at the costs associated with joining each networking group and ask yourself what the likelihood is of you recouping these costs through generating new clients and new business from the members. Now, ask the same question of yourself. What is the likelihood of you being able to generate new clients and new business for the members? You may find it useful to write your answers down before making any commitment. Finally, make your decision to join the group that appears to be most appropriate to yourself and your business.

"Being honest, professional and natural at all times works best for me, even when individuals aren't obvious bedfellows. Make a memorable impression and one person can refer you to another. So always be courteous, make sure they know what you do and move on when the time is right. My business name usually raises an eyebrow and this allows me to explain what we do whilst the listener is still smiling."

Steph Savill, Director FOXY Lady Drivers Club

Attending Networking Events

Joining a networking group where you get together with other business people on a weekly or monthly basis doesn't stop you from attending other networking events that are organised on a more informal basis. It is not that difficult to find out what networking events are taking place in your area. Once you start networking, you will suddenly become the recipient of dozens of invitations through word-of-mouth, e-mail and direct mail. If you're keen to explore what's happening locally, then local business magazines and local district websites plus your Chamber of Commerce are all good places to start.

It's easy to get carried away with the enjoyment of networking and before you know it, your week can be dotted with networking events that you have to fit your work around. This is not something that I would advise. Your time is money and it needs to be spent wisely.

Make sure that you evaluate each networking event before committing to it. Is it a worthwhile use of your time? Why are you going to it? Who will be there? Sometimes it's worth attending a networking event simply to listen to a good speaker or to recharge your batteries. Don't become so relaxed when you are networking that you behave as though you're in the company of good friends on a Friday night. Over-indulging with alcohol or telling jokes more appropriate for friends and family should be avoided if you want to build a great reputation.

"Networking has been a very important means of developing my business. My approach has always been to get to know networking colleagues on a personal basis as in my opinion people do business with people rather than with businesses. Knowing someone personally is key in terms of finding out what makes them tick and how they can be more effective in creating networking opportunities for me. Likewise, it helps me better understand how I can help them."

Marco Vallone, Independent Financial Adviser

How to Benefit from Online Business Networking

So far, we've been looking at the benefits of face-to-face networking, but let's now consider the use of online networking. Online business networking can be a powerful and time efficient method of promoting your business. In fact, the beauty of online networking is that you can network at any time of the day or night, and on any day of the week. If you work on your own then online networking is a great way to engage with people when you have only a few minutes to spare and you don't want to leave the office. I am active in both online and face-to-face networking, although I do get most of my business through the latter. Here's what online networking expert and small business entrepreneur, Nick Broom, has to say about the subject.

" If you're a small business, there's a fair chance that you have built your business largely on reputation, through the power of word of

mouth and recommendation. And I'll bet that along the way, you've shared something, whether that is your knowledge or your contacts, with your own group of contacts. As the Web matures, there are an increasing range of online tools at your disposal that can help you to cast your net wider and you don't need to be an IT expert or even spend anything to take part.

There are some very important guidelines about these new forms of engagement that the big brands have trouble with, but small businesses can easily implement with great results. First of all, think about your markets and the web sites they may use – if you make or sell consumer goods, then Facebook (www.facebook.com) may be a good place where consumers gather. If you provide services, then LinkedIn (www.linkedin.com) may be more appropriate. If in doubt, ask your customers. Set up accounts on the websites that are most appropriate, and if possible, set up user or loyalty groups. You can then start talking to your network online.

Next, start to think about your strategy to engage people. It's no use simply registering and waiting for people to come to you. You need to provide a reason, share some insight, knowledge or tips with the audience, and then direct them from your other communications.

Make sure you are:

- o *Consistent. Set up your online brand in the same way on all of the websites you use*
- o *Yourself. Being authentic and credible will win you friends*
- o *Honest*
- o *Unique (don't just re-type what others write)*

If you follow these simple rules, you will build increasing trust in your online brand. If you are consistent and provide interest, expertise and value to your audience, you will increase your network and raise awareness of your expertise or products, just as you do in the offline world."

Here are some tips that will help you network online:

- **Find professional networks that cover your sector.** There can be a value in talking online with other professionals that do what you do. You can build your business profile; share good practice and find out what is happening within your peer community at large.

- **Find the forums where you can connect** with potential clients and network with other professionals. Like Nick, I also use LinkedIn as a way of showcasing my experience and my work availability. This is really useful when a potential client is trying to search for information about me online. At the same time, I can make connections with other business people that may not have a need for my services, but through knowing what I do can recommend me. Other business people that I know network online with ecademy. (*www.ecademy.com*). Do your research and choose the online networks that are most suitable for you.

- **Build a positive profile online where you establish** yourself as an expert. I contribute marketing articles to Enterprise Nation (*www.enterprisenation.com*) and I join in the discussion forums on a regular basis, dispensing marketing advice freely. Be genuine and helpful so that the online community trusts and respects you. Journalists are increasingly scanning websites on the lookout for interesting case studies. You could be approached by one of them for a story simply because it is clear from the forum discussions that you are an expert. The BBC initially found me via a blog.

- **Be regular and be consistent.** Find a few good online networks where you can build your profile and where you can focus on giving and sharing, as well as gaining. By joining an online community and contributing to it on a regular basis, you will raise your profile with the search engines.

- **Pause before you post any advice or add your opinion** to an existing discussion or article. Unlike face-to-face networking where people can see you, when you contribute to an online forum you are judged purely by the content and tone of your contributions. If your responses are strewn with spelling mistakes then you are unlikely to create a good impression. If you are taking a controversial stand on a topic, you must be confident that your words will neither land you in hot water nor alienate the online community. Read through your contributions before you press the send button!

- **Be in it for the long haul.** When you have found the right online networks, focus on being genuine, honest and helpful. Aim to build relationships over a period of time just as you would with face-to-face networking. Become a person that other people can look to for great commentary and advice, or even a touch of humour. You will be pleasantly surprised with the results.

"Networking online is becoming as important as networking face-to-face. And the best thing is, you can meet hundreds more contacts without stepping out of your home office! So how to successfully network online? Find the space that works best for you; this could be a combination of free apps like Twitter (twitter.com) contact systems such as LinkedIn or business sites like my own at www. enterprisenation.com. Spend time in that space and get to know the community that hangs out there. Share your knowledge, show your

expertise, help out community members and before you know it, this will convert into opportunities and leads. Spending time online will lead to new business offline."

Emma Jones, Director and founder of Enterprise Nation

The Common Types of Networker

After attending numerous networking events and groups over the years, it soon became apparent to me that although there are different styles of networking, many fall into the four categories below. I can guarantee that you'll come across members of each category within any networking group that you visit and any networking event that you attend.

1. **The Hunter** - this is the person that presents you with their business card within seconds of meeting you. They then proceed to fire questions at you, wanting to know what you do and the types of clients you work with. Within minutes they are either turning on their heel to find the next person to interrogate or they're asking for introductions to your clients. Best avoided at all costs as they are only in it for themselves.

2. **The Gatherer** - this person sells a product or service for which most other businesses have a need, for example office supplies. It is therefore easy for you to introduce your clients to them. When it comes to getting business for you however they don't seem to go that extra mile and push themselves for your benefit. It tends to be a one-way relationship.

3. **The Invisible Networker**- this is the person that joins a networking group or attends a regular networking event

and yet you hardly notice they are there. They appear to be timid and shy away from contact with other group members. They know that they need to network but seem reluctant to do so. They neither give nor take from the group and tend not to renew their membership after the first year - usually because they are disillusioned or simply baffled at the lack of hot leads.

4. **The All-Rounder** - this is the person we should seek out and indeed aspire to become. The All-Rounder focuses upon actively seeking business opportunities for their fellow networkers. They have a 'referral radar' which means that when they are out and about doing business on a daily basis, they are also looking for great leads and introductions for their fellow members. And yet by concentrating on finding referrals for other group members, they also receive a high proportion of referrals themselves. (The very apt BNI description of this is ' givers gain') All-Rounders tend to be enthusiastic and positive about the whole networking process. They regard networking as an enjoyable and productive part of their working day. They pitch up early, help out with the arrangements and stay on afterwards engaging in one-to-one conversations with their fellow members. Networking works for them, because they commit themselves wholeheartedly to the process.

The good news is that if you aim to be an All-Rounder but you believe that you are not quite there yet, recognising that you still have work to do is a step in the right direction. In the rest of this chapter, we look at the skills that are needed to help you become that All-Rounder.

"Networking is widely acknowledged as one of the most effective ways of gathering information, building relationships and spotting

opportunities. For me, the key to networking success is being positive. No one likes a moaner (apart from another moaner that is) so I always charge myself up to bring some good news into the room and I focus on the positive aspects of business. Also, recognise that networking is a long-term investment and it's simply unrealistic to sell on the day. Set time aside to build your profile through regular attendance. Oh, and keep smiling (people will wonder why!)"

Tim Fifield, Director of Business Builder Club

How to Be Remembered for All the Right Reasons

Once you start marketing your business through networking, you will need to approach it with enthusiasm, focus and passion. Joining a group where you stand in the corner like a wallflower every week, hoping that people will talk to you, will not win you advocates and hot leads.

People have to get to know you and to know that you care about their business as well as your own. They will then start to feel comfortable recommending you. You need to demonstrate that you can deliver on your promises by following up on any recommendation in a professional and positive manner. Here are some further tips that will help you become that All-Rounder:

- **Rapport comes before referrals!** People are going to like you, based on how you make them feel about themselves. If people feel happy and positive in your presence, then it's quite natural that they will want to recommend your business to potential clients. You can build genuine rapport by showing an interest in the person you are speaking to. Don't automatically respond to something that they say with one of your own experiences. Get them to expand by asking questions. As the great Dale Carnegie wrote in his book *How to Win Friends and Influence People*, "You can make more friends in two months by becoming interested in other people than you can in two years by trying to get other people interested in you."

- **Give people your time.** How do you feel when the person that you are talking to is looking over your shoulder or fiddling with their mobile phone? It's inevitable that some of the people you meet will never be in a position to recommend you. However if you focus on being gracious to everybody, listening to what they are saying and maintaining eye contact, then you will build an enviable reputation.

- **Use positive and welcoming body language.** A warm and friendly smile, accompanied by a relaxed open posture, tells people that you are approachable and welcoming. This will have a positive effect on the people in your presence. Remember to nod, to acknowledge what is being said and to be enthusiastic (where appropriate). As a leading psychologist said, "People who smile tend to manage, teach and sell more effectively". Try to avoid frowning, crossing your arms and yawning.

"So what makes for a good networker? This is something that I am asked on countless occasions. I believe that dieting is the answer! Successful networking is like dieting in that it doesn't happen all at once. I attend many meetings where people are trying to do that big deal on the evening at the first asking, whereas they should be seeing it as the start of the ongoing relationship. People buy people in the first instance and not necessarily the product or service. Happy dieting!"

Richard Dandy, Chairman of the Surrey Hills East branch of the Federation of Small Businesses and Ambassador for BNI in Sussex

- **Have some useful conversation starters to hand.** Knowing how to take the lead and start a conversation is important – it avoids that awkward silent period when you have gathered together in a small group. Whoever said that silence is golden should have added 'and it can be uncomfortable too.' I have attended countless networking events when a silence has descended upon the group of people that I am with. When this happens it will help if you can bring the quieter members into the conversation. Ask for their views on what has been said. Try to use conversation starters that everyone can contribute to.

    o "So how are you finding business conditions at the moment?"

    o "How many networking events do you attend?"

    o "Did you read/see the article on…?"

    o "How useful is the Internet for promoting your business?"

    o "How long have you been attending this networking group?"

    o "What is your line of business?"

    o "This seems like a really successful networking group"

    o "How long have you been in your line of business?"

- **Be considerate** when you want to move from the person that you are talking to. You can for example:

o Make an excuse for a loo break, explain that you need to get something from your briefcase or your car or, simply say, "Would you excuse me for a moment, I need to catch up with…"

o Say, "It's been great talking to you but I suppose we need to network and move on. Hopefully we will get the chance to catch up again later."

o Introduce the person to someone else. This is important if you are attending your regular networking group and talking to a visitor who doesn't know many of the members. Walking up to a group of complete strangers can be daunting for the best of us.

- **Try to find common ground.** It is easier to form a connection with a person if you can find a mutual interest or acquaintance. Look for ways to connect and identify with the individuals in your networking group and the people at the events you attend, and make a note to remember what links you. What connects you will vary from person to person – it could be your shared perception of current business conditions, but just as easily it could be a love of the same sport, your children, your outlook on life. Not every conversation has to focus on work related matters.

"In my experience, the top three traits of a successful networker are: they turn up, they turn up again and guess what, yes they turn up again! We run women's business clubs all over the country and it's fair to say that I've met every type of networker going. I believe that people buy people. Prospective customers and business contacts are more likely to use "Jane, who is a great person and also an accountant" rather than just "Jane, the accountant". It's too easy at a business event to focus completely on what you are rather than who you are. I also think that although elevator pitches are really useful and they have

their place at business and networking events, sometimes they can be overused. What should be a simple 'hello' becomes an unpleasantly intense sales pitch. When you're meeting someone for the first time, simply tell them your name and save your elevator pitch for when they ask you what you do."

Kelly Stevens, Founder, The Women's Business Clubs
(www.thewomensbusinessclubs.com)

- **Be genuine in your enthusiasm and praise.** Everyone loves to be appreciated. If you can make a point of giving some genuine praise to your fellow networkers and showing an interest in what they are saying to you, then you will win many ambassadors for your business. So, if a member entertains you with a good stand up presentation – tell them. If you are given a good lead, thank the member personally and tell the group. If you have received some positive feedback on a member, convey this to them. If you have enjoyed talking to someone that you have not met before, let him or her know this. Look for opportunities where you can make a positive impact.

- **Follow through promptly on the recommendations** that you are given and when you get a sale, make sure that you communicate your gratitude to the person responsible and to the group. A public thank you can be more powerful than a private one.

Your One-Minute Chance to Shine

At many networking events and meetings you are usually given 60 seconds to explain what you do to your captive audience. The reality is that many people will be focusing on their own presentation or will not be concentrating properly because the previous 60 seconds were boring. How many times have you attended a networking event where someone has stood up and talked about their business and you are still none the wiser? It's important that you are clear and concise when you are describing what you do if you want people to recommend you. Building a good reputation and being on the receiving end of great referrals entails preparing and delivering a presentation that will really grab the attention of your audience. Use the following guide to explain what you do (I've used one of my 60 second presentations by way of illustration):

- **Your business name**

"Good morning everybody my name is Dee Blick from The Marketing Gym Ltd."

- **Anything that is special and different about you or your business**

"I am an award-winning Chartered Marketer with 24 years of practical hands-on marketing experience and I've recently written a book called Powerful Marketing on a Shoestring Budget for Small Businesses."

- **In a few sentences, what you offer and the benefits**

"I work with many small businesses delivering measurable results on a shoestring budget. This includes small and well-crafted direct mail campaigns, powerful PR coverage in targeted media and award-winning copywriting newsletters, brochures, websites and adverts."

- **In a few sentences what you are looking for**

"I am running my 'PR on a Shoestring' workshops through Business Link in September and October. If you would like to book a free place,

or know a small-business owner that would welcome the opportunity of some PR training, take my business card or book now!"

- **Your sign off**

"So, that is Dee Blick from The Marketing Gym Ltd making your business leaner, fitter and more powerful - on a shoestring budget."

Spend time sketching out what you want to say and then practice until you sound natural and confident. If you are not confident enough to deliver your 60 seconds without notes, use a cue card with your key bullet points rather than a flimsy sheet of paper. You will find it difficult to connect with your audience if you have a piece of paper covering up your face.

Resist the temptation to repeat the same one- minute presentation week in week out. People will get bored and you will get bored too. People that are successful at networking tend to vary what they say so that their audience doesn't switch off the moment they open their mouth. Why not use your 60 seconds to share some positive customer feedback or a really interesting case study? Don't try and cram too much detail into your 60 seconds. Focus on key bullet points and bring passion into what you are saying.

Consider using props to add interest to your presentation. Why not make people sit up and pay attention to your presentation by using some of the tools of your trade. Here are a few examples that I have seen at networking events:

- o An editor showing copies of her magazine and highlighting one article inside.

- o A Web developer with project boards of a stunning website that he designed and built.

o A telemarketing trainer delivering her 60-second presentations using a telephone.

o The Director of a signage company demonstrating his latest pop-up banners and how they can be assembled in seconds.

o A business owner showing two bags full of shredded documents to promote his document shredding service.

o A florist holding two of her stunning bouquets and describing them beautifully.

Don't just rely on your voice and body language for impact. Plan your presentations a month ahead and think about how you can make them memorable.

"I believe that being prepared before I go to a networking event is important. So, I make sure that I have plenty of business cards with me and that I have a good idea of what I'm going to say when I get there."

Katrina Smith, Managing Director True Colours Interiors

Measuring the Impact of Your Networking

Successful networkers know that attending regular networking meetings and networking events is the beginning of the new business process. Going one step further and converting those leads into sales takes real commitment.

- **Make sure that you always take accurate** and detailed notes when you are given a referral. Ask questions about the warm lead you are being given. What are they expecting from you? What has already been said about you? When do they want you to get in touch? How would they like you to contact them?

- **Make sure that you follow up on warm leads** as soon as possible. There's nothing worse than the person who has gone to the time and trouble of warming up a great lead for you finding out that you haven't made contact several days later.

- **When you actually get the work, make sure that you** deliver to your highest standards. You want the person that initially recommended you to be on the receiving end of positive feedback from the person that you have done the work for.

- **Make a note of all the business that you obtain** from networking and contrast this with your networking costs. Are you acquiring decent quality new business at a low acquisition cost? Keep a record. This will make you even more focused when you are networking and you'll be able to compare the effectiveness of networking with your other marketing activities.

At the end of the day, successful networking on a shoestring is all about commitment, enthusiasm, integrity and attention to every single detail. But remember to have fun along the way too!

3 HOW TO TURN A COLD CALL INTO A WARM LEAD

The telephone is one of the most effective tools that you can use to build relationships with potential clients. But for many people the thought of picking up the telephone and making an introduction to another person they've never spoken to before is not a pleasant one. It's not quite up there with the fear of public speaking, but it's close. We find it easier to retreat behind e-mails that although quick and easy to fire off are not enough when it comes to building relationships.

So why am I an advocate of telephone cold calling for small businesses? 10 years ago I was recruited by a training business with the task of signing up 200 new clients for their insurance training services. The only marketing tool at my disposal was the telephone. The idea was that when I had mastered the art of making cold calls, I would train a small team to continue with what I had started.

After spending one morning on the telephone, trying in vain to arrange meetings with potential clients, I was ready to throw in the towel. Despite years of experience in the insurance sector I really didn't know how to connect with the person at the end of the telephone. The minute I hit an objection, I would bid a hasty retreat. I knew that I needed to change my approach but was not sure how. I therefore embarked on an intensive two-week period of studying successful telephone techniques, practising until I was blue in the face.

With a new and improved attitude, I began quickly to get results, the business targets were met and I progressed to developing an intensive one-day telephone cold calling workshop. This has since been delivered to hundreds of business people ranging from Directors of multi-million pound companies to sole traders and new start-ups.

In this chapter, I'm going to share with you the tips, experience and strategies that I include in my one-day workshop. They should go a long way towards enabling you to build relationships from a cold start. So, what are we going to cover?

- The difference between the traditional telesales approach and the relationship building approach
- The importance of preparation - setting objectives, who are you going to call, storing your data, clearing your diary, finding your space
- Communicating benefits without a script
- Top tips on voice and body language
- Let me introduce you to the gatekeeper
- You're through! How to make a powerful introduction
- How to handle those initial objections
- Building rapport - asking questions, listening, paying genuine compliments
- Building up to a positive finish
- Tips for using a telemarketing business to make your cold calls
- Measure your success on a regular basis

The Difference Between the Traditional Telesales Approach and the Relationship Building Approach

You're at work, and the phone rings. At the other end is a cheerful voice, announcing in script like tones that their product or service is going to take your business into the next league. It's no good trying to say anything because they're in full flow. When you get a moment to interrupt, you let them know that you're very busy and that you don't need their product or services (even if you do). You feel irritated at being disturbed and this reinforces your dislike of receiving telesales calls and of making telephone cold calls yourself.

When you use the telephone to build relationships, you accept that the process takes time, commitment and trust. For example in a first introductory call you will be trying to determine if this person has a genuine need for what you have to offer before you even think about moving to the next stage with them. This is different from the traditional telesales approach where the aim is to make as many phone calls as possible in as short a space of time as possible, in the hope that someone reluctantly agrees to a meeting or a sale.

Manage your expectations

- o The telephone can play a big part in opening the door to a potential sale, but it's rarely a one hit wonder.

- o Developing profitable business relationships with potential new clients from a cold start will probably entail several phone calls, augmented with your marketing literature, e-mails and meetings.

o Don't become downhearted by rejection. The road to cold calling success is definitely paved with rejections. This is the nature of the beast. If you expect every call to be successful then you will be disappointed. Focus on remaining upbeat and pushing through the rejections because you will come away with positive results.

Think about it. How many sales have you made where you sat back and did nothing? Don't expect that first cold telephone call to yield miracles – yet it's a great door opener, a vital link that takes your prospect from having no awareness of your business to being aware and interested.

The Importance of Preparation - Setting Objectives

At a practical level, setting objectives actually starts you thinking about your business and what you would like a particular marketing activity to deliver. One of the big advantages of objective setting is that you establish realistic goals that you can work towards. Measuring your performance as you work towards achieving these goals is motivational. Consider what you want cold calling to achieve for your business.

To help you, here is a selection of objectives that were generated by delegates on my workshops:

o We want to bring on board two new clients each month where the initial introduction has been made on the telephone.

o We want to target 1000 of the small-business owners on our database over the next year using the telephone to make the first introduction.

○ We want to secure meetings with 100 design agencies and marketing companies in the county in the next 12 months. We will use the telephone to introduce ourselves so that when our direct mail arrives, it won't be dismissed out of hand.

○ We want to make 12 to 15 phone calls every single month in which we ask Motability car dealerships to visit our new website and give their feedback on it.

Different businesses have different objectives. If you have not been successful at telephone cold calling before, or if this is your first toe in the water, it's very difficult to create sales targets that are meaningful.

In my experience, rather than focusing on how many sales you'd like your cold calling to generate, why not establish specific activity targets such as these workshop examples?

Over a period of time you will get a feeling for how many sales are coming through from your cold calling. Then you can establish some realistic sales targets because they will be based on your actual experience of telephone cold calling rather than an uninformed guess. Often at my workshops, delegates arrive feeling disillusioned that they have not achieved their unrealistic sales targets. When we start to focus on their levels of activity, and the need to commit to establishing activity goals they become re-energised, understanding the need for preparation.

So, first of all, decide on your activity objectives for cold calling. It is when you have a good understanding of the number of actual sales that are coming through from this activity that you should set your sales objectives. For some businesses, it's relatively straightforward to generate sales through telephone cold calling in a short timeframe. For others, the decision-making process takes longer. It could be several months before a sale is concluded. Because of this, only you can establish realistic activity targets and equally realistic sales targets.

The Importance of Preparation - Who Are You Going to Call?

Good-quality, accurate data is the bedrock of effective cold calling. You don't want to spend valuable time only to encounter many irate responses because the data that you are using is old and incorrect. There are a number of ways that you can source data.

- **If you have accumulated piles of business cards** on your travels from people that you would like to do business with, this can be a good place to start. However, if you've been holding on to a business card for more than three months, the information could have changed and you will need to check beforehand. In future, when you take a business card make sure that you ask the person's permission to call them so that you keep within the laws that govern telephone cold calling. (More on this later)

- **You can build your own list of contacts** by searching the many online and offline directories available, and trawling your targeted business magazines, for businesses that you would like to contact. It is unlikely that this will yield the full details of the person that you need to speak to, so an extra telephone call will be required to establish this information. Ask the receptionist (often referred to as the gatekeeper) if the details that you have sourced are still valid. You don't often encounter gatekeeper resistance at this stage and it's a low-cost and reliable way of adding vital data to the information that you have already gathered. However, the gatekeeper may well tell you that it is company policy not to take cold calls. If this is the case, you should remove the contact from your list.

- **If you have bought a list of cold prospects** and it's now several months old, you need to be aware of the Telephone Preference Service and the Corporate Telephone Preference Service (*www.tpsonline.org.uk*). Businesses that have registered with one of these two services in any calendar month should not receive further cold calls. It is then the responsibility of organisations that sell and rent lists to make sure that their lists are updated and that new subscribers to the Telephone Preference Services are removed from them. By using data that is more than one month old, you run the risk of being reported to the Data Protection Commissioner for making cold calls to businesses that have chosen not to receive any. Whilst the chances of this happening are quite slender, it makes good business sense to work from squeaky-clean data. You don't want to target businesses that don't want to receive your calls. Be aware of this when making calls from old lists. You may have to make an apology and back out of the call, making sure that you subsequently flag this record as being 'no contact'.

- **If your data is several months old,** the chances are that a significant percentage of it will be incorrect. If you don't have the time to clean your data then it's a good idea for both legal and commercial reasons to pay someone to do this for you.

- **There are many reputable organisations** from which lists can be rented or data downloaded where every month the data is cleaned to ensure it complies with the Telephone Preference Services. One of these organisations, Thomson Directories, offers a superb low-cost online search and data download system called Business Search PRO (*www. businessstrata.com*) that is ideal for many small businesses.

If you're looking to rent or buy data, then read Chapter 4 where this subject is covered in some detail.

The Importance of Preparation - Storing Your Data

When you start cold calling, you should take notes of the important details from each conversation. When you follow-up with another telephone call, reading through these notes beforehand will remind you of your previous conversation.

If cold calling is to form a significant role in your marketing strategy, then it's a good idea to invest in a contact management system such as ACT. With these systems, you will be able to access individual records, together with the details of all of your previous conversations, immediately. Before you sign up to any system however, ask for a free demonstration and a free trial run. You will then be able to make an informed choice from the various options.

If investing in one of these systems is outside of your current budget, then invest in some decent files and build an efficient paper-based system. The main thing is that you hold thorough, accurate and up-to-date records on every person that you contact.

The Importance of Preparation - Clearing Your Diary

Without a doubt, one of the biggest reasons why small businesses fail to harness the power of the telephone at building warm relationships is a lack of commitment rather than a lack of skill. You can have the best telephone manner in the world and the most compelling messages about your business, but if you haven't made time in your diary to make those calls they won't happen.

Booking time in your diary to make those cold calls is fundamental. Successful businesses go one step further and allocate calling slots over a four-week period. If you know that every single week there is time in your diary for cold calling, then you're much more likely to commit to it. If you approach the whole process with the attitude of "I'll do it, when I get the odd spare hour" the chances are that your spare hour will never materialise. Earlier we covered the importance of setting objectives. Your objectives can only be met if you allocate enough time to achieve them. When you start making cold calls you will soon find out whether you have allocated sufficient time to meet your targets or whether you need more.

When you actually use the time allocated in your diary to make cold calls, something amazing happens.

- o Because you're talking to cold prospects on a regular basis, you will begin to sound confident and enthusiastic and there's nothing like a naturally enthusiastic person for securing leads.

- o Your natural fear of rejection starts to fade and is replaced by an anticipation of success. You consequently become even more motivated to make those calls.

- o You become familiar with how to respond to objections in a confident and experienced way. Nothing unsettles you as you have heard them all before.

- o You understand how to structure and conduct a call so that your cold prospect is inspired to move to the next stage.

In short, because you have committed to the cold calling process by setting aside regular time in your diary, you have become 'a natural' on the telephone. It's this natural, non-pressured approach that will win you warm leads, hot meetings and sales!

How much time should you set aside?

If you can set aside as little as one 3-hour session every single week, then you will be off to a flying start. The odd half hour here and there will not yield the same results. That's because for the first 30 minutes of calling you're getting into your stride.

If, after 3 hours you have emerged with three meaningful conversations that have led to confirmed meetings, or have gone some way towards establishing a warm relationship with a handful of previous cold prospects, then you can look upon the session as a successful one.

If you have a business where it's a real challenge to reach a decision maker, your initial calls will be focused on finding out names and locations. Emerging with names that you can target in a subsequent session is another example of an effective use of your time on the telephone.

Remember, unlike the telesales approach, this is not about aiming to get through as many phone calls as possible. It's about getting through to the people that you know have a deep need for your products and services. Once you have their attention, it's about opening the door to a potential sale. So to conclude

- **Start by setting aside a minimum** of three hours every single week for at least three consecutive months to really get into your stride and build a positive momentum.

- **Block this time out in your diary** and approach it with the same commitment that you would give to a meeting with an important client, by only cancelling if unavoidable.

The Importance of Preparation - Finding Your Space

When I was immersed in my research on how to become a skilled telephone cold caller, I found that discussing in which environment telephone calls should be made attracted many different views. Some books would suggest that making cold calls from a busy office environment was fine, whereas others would recommend finding a completely private and quiet space. Ultimately, it's down to you to determine which environment you prefer but here are 4 tips that may help you:

- **In your early weeks of telephone cold calling,** you're likely to feel self-conscious that other people can hear what you are saying. This will impact your performance because you will be worrying about what your colleagues are thinking rather than concentrating fully. If you work in an office environment with other people and a private space is out of the question, try to find a screen that provides some separation. Consider placing a sign on it saying, "do not interrupt - on the phone." For many business people that I have trained, this seems to be a workable compromise between a private office space and a noisy office environment.

- **It's worth bearing in mind that even if cold calling** in a noisy office environment does not distract you, the chances are that the person on the end of the phone will be able to hear the background noise and this may disturb them or even impact on their ability to hear you. This doesn't sound professional and it tends to be the signature tune of the telesales caller.

- **If you are a home-based business and you work on your own** then you don't have to worry about moving away from noisy team members. However, you do have other challenges! Depending on where you work at home, you have to be aware that all types of background noise can come through quite clearly to the person you're calling. A washing machine in its full spin cycle can be very noisy. Your dog barking in the background can be a distraction too. Your partner coming into the room and asking an innocent question can really throw you off your train of thought. So try to organise a degree of separation before starting the calls.

- **You have to be disciplined and stick to the task at hand**. Don't answer the door if the doorbell rings. Now is not the time to demonstrate your ability to multitask. If you were talking to a cold prospect in person, you would give them your full attention and you need to do the same on the telephone.

So take a good look at your work environment and make these positive changes before you even pick up the phone.

Communicating Benefits Without a Script

The scripted call is another hallmark of the telesales caller. You instinctively know when someone calls you whether they're reading from a script or not. Scripts are for actors learning their lines. When it comes to building successful relationships on the telephone with cold prospects, don't use one. Even if you sound confident and accomplished, which is unlikely, the moment an interruption comes your way it will be difficult to return to the script. It will probably need to be abandoned, causing confusion all round. That's not to say that you shouldn't use prompt notes to help you. Later in the chapter, I'm going to share with you a powerful capsule introduction and some equally strong techniques to use when handling objections. By all means, type these out in full and spend time becoming familiar with them. But when you go live, use them only for reference. It's important to speak in a natural and confident manner about the benefits that you can offer. This is what potential clients are looking for. They want to hear that you have solutions to their problems before they will open up and really listen to you. So, grab a sheet of A4 and aim to fill it with 10 benefits. What should your benefit sheet include?

- **Focus on why your existing clients came to you** initially and why they continue to use you. If you are in doubt, call a few of them and ask. You can include the best responses in your benefit sheet.

- **Add some compelling and accurate facts** about your products or services. .... 'We are the only provider of this bespoke software in the county'.... 'We provide our print services for the top three design agencies in the UK and they've been using us for the past two years'.... 'We have a no strings guarantee that if you don't recoup the cost of our marketing services within four weeks, we return your fees in full'. Write down 3 to 6 great facts to which you can refer during the conversation.

- **With regard to your happy clients,** can you share something incredible that you have done for each one of them? People are interested in finding out what you have achieved for similar clients and providing some strong examples may help to secure that meeting. It's easy to forget these examples, however, if you don't have a benefit sheet to prompt you.

Top Tips on Voice and Body Language

Until I came across this statistic, *83% of us judge a person on the phone by their tone of voice,* I hadn't given much thought to my voice and how it sounded on the telephone. Our voice and how we use it is our sole communication tool on the telephone. In a face-to-face situation, the person we are speaking with can look at us and tell whether we are fully engaged with them. We make constant eye contact, and mirror their positive body language. We smile and nod as appropriate - our voice is just one method of communication available to us. On the telephone this is not the case and as a result, our voice has to work really hard. Here are some tips on how to use your voice and body language effectively on the telephone:

- **Buying a dicta-phone** is a simple but effective way to find out how you sound. When you are able to listen to yourself without cringing, use it to practice new skills and to ensure that your voice sounds natural and interesting.

- **Enthusiasm is vital.** How can you communicate your enthusiasm on the telephone without sounding as though you've had a sharp intake of helium? Emphasising key words is the answer. Be careful not to overdo it but emphasising a few key words in each sentence will have a positive impact. "That's a *really* interesting point that you have just made" "This system is *incredibly powerful*" "We are currently saving businesses *an amazing 60%* on their telephone bills."

- **Don't try to suppress your accent, but be aware of your speed.** Regional accents are fantastic and diversity is always attractive. However if you are a fast talker, you will have to practice slowing down or you will lose people early in the conversation. The same is true if you're a slow talker. You run the risk that you will lose people if they become bored and irritated while waiting for a point to be made.

- **Think of your voice as a flowing and meandering stream.** Vary your tone so that your voice goes up and down, with emphasis on key points and plenty of very short but powerful pauses to demonstrate confidence in your message. Again it's so important to practice and listen to how you sound. It is then much easier to make changes.

- **Try not to 'umm and err'** when you speak on the telephone. Be aware of this natural tendency that we all share and make a conscious effort to.............. pause instead. You will sound more professional, and you will feel altogether calmer.

- **Do you need to adjust your volume?** If you're used to speaking loudly, this will not do you any favours on the telephone. You will sound intimidating. Imagine you have a volume switch and when you're on the phone, picture yourself turning your volume down. Of course the opposite is also true if you are naturally very quietly spoken.

- **It's important that you focus on the quality** of your breathing in your early days of cold calling when you are more likely to feel nervous. Before you pick up the telephone, practice breathing from your middle, taking oxygen through your nose rather than your mouth. This will make your voice sound more powerful and steady when you are talking. Anxiety can sometimes make us sound breathless so if this happens, focus on breathing slowly and steadily until the nerves die down.

- **Your body language has a bigger part** to play in your success on the telephone than you think. Don't hunch over your desk because this will suppress your tone. Similarly clutching the telephone to your ear while trying to scan your screen will make you sound distracted. Relax your shoulders and adopt a comfortable and natural posture. Try to imagine that the person you are going to speak to is actually in front of you.

- **Always smile** before picking up the telephone to make a cold call. It's a fact that when we smile, we release positive endorphins that make us feel good. If you feel positive then you will sound positive.

- **Don't engage in these common distraction** behaviours on the telephone…fiddling with your hair or jewellery, clicking your pen, playing with your mobile phone. If you're planning on eating a snack or drinking a cup of coffee, save it for when your conversation has ended. Remember, your body language and your state of alertness can make a hugely positive contribution to every single call that you make. It's amazing what the person at the end of the phone can hear and they may not tell you that your obvious distraction and the accompanying background noise is the reason why they don't want to carry on talking to you.

Let Me Introduce You to the Gatekeeper

When I first started cold calling, I didn't realise the power of the receptionist or the personal assistant. On numerous occasions it was their decision whether I was transferred through or politely declined. So, after experiencing several rejections from these 'gatekeepers' I knew that change was needed. You may have the most effective telephone skills in the world at the ready to impress your potential client, but if you can't overcome the first hurdle of getting past the gatekeeper, you're scuppered.

First of all, you need to be aware of the three main types of gatekeeper that you're likely going to come across:

- **The "forget it, punk!" gatekeeper**. You can be fantastic on the telephone but no cold calls are going to be put through. Why? Because it's company policy to bar cold calls and the business will in all likelihood have registered with one of the Telephone Preference Services. When you're faced with this immediate rejection, you have to find another route into the company. Ask the people at your networking group if they can give you a contact in that company. Or how about composing an attention grabbing direct mailshot?

- **The "tell me more" gatekeeper**. You are definitely in with a shout here. This gatekeeper is like a Doctor's receptionist. They want to know more about why you're calling. Depending on what you say and how you say it, they will make a decision on whether to put you through or politely turn you away.

- **The "just putting you through" gatekeeper**. Before you have even finished the surname of the person you want to speak to, you are through. It's wonderful when this happens and reassuring to know that these type of gatekeepers still exist.

Here are some suggestions for when you're faced with the "tell me more" gatekeeper:

- **Always greet the gatekeeper with 'good morning',** 'good afternoon' or simply a warm and friendly 'hello', followed by your full name and company name. If you are a local business and the business you're calling is local too, mention this – it creates an immediate bond and the gatekeeper may even recognise your business.

- **If you don't know the name of the person** that you want to speak to, ask for help. If you are then asked why you're calling avoid a rambling speech about your business. Explain that you would like to introduce yourself to this particular person because you believe that your products or services will be of genuine interest to them. If you work with similar businesses, mention this. Don't volunteer any more information at this stage.

- **If the suggestion is made that you post some information** instead (a great way to get you off the phone) explain that you try not to send out unwanted mail and you find that customers often appreciate a brief courtesy call beforehand. Mention that you are not a telesales executive. This is your business and you intend only to make a brief introduction. I still make cold calls every single month and find this to be a really effective approach.

- **If the gatekeeper sounds harassed or busy** make an empathetic comment " I'm sorry to bother you when you sound like you're having a busy day." Don't most of us like a little attention? If you sound genuine it will make it harder for the gatekeeper to decline your call.

- **If the gatekeeper is helpful, make a point of thanking them**. If you get a warm greeting from the person that you're put through to, tell them how professional and helpful the gatekeeper was. Most of us like to be on the receiving end of positive feedback. You should aim to build a positive impression of yourself and your business with every person in the organisation that you come into contact with.

- **Make a note of the gatekeeper's name.** Better still ask for it. When you call again, if it's the same gatekeeper, you can build on the rapport that you established in the first telephone call. If it's a different person, then referencing your earlier phone call by including the name of the gatekeeper shows that you are not making a cold call and have had previous contact with the company. This should also remove the need for you to run through your introductory chat again before being put through.

It is vital that you are friendly and courteous to whomever you deal with and the gatekeeper is no exception. Remember, the gatekeeper has the power to make or break a potential sale. If you approach this important first stage of the telephone cold calling process in a hurry or you treat the gatekeeper as an unwelcome irritant, then your chances of success will nosedive.

At the same time don't become disheartened if, despite your very best efforts, you are still not put through. Your magic can't work on every gatekeeper and there will always be some that will not succumb, no matter how pleasant and articulate you are. Continue to be polite in the face of rejection and move on to the next call.

You're Through! How to Make a Powerful Introduction

The gatekeeper has just put you through and at the end of the line is the person that you really want to speak to. You haven't spoken before so you're feeling a little apprehensive but pleased that you are now in with a chance.

You know that what you say in the next few seconds and how you say it is so important. Look back over the many telesales calls that you have undoubtedly received during your lifetime and the chances are that the introductions followed a standard format. Usually a very brief hello, followed by the name of the person calling you, followed by a lengthy, scripted talk about their products and why you should be buying them.

This is not an introduction that I would advise you copy or adopt. You're looking to build an intelligent and mutually beneficial relationship from a cold start. Your introduction is the start of the relationship building process and as such, it has to be professional, articulate and empowering. Here is a capsule introduction that I developed many years ago. It stands me in good stead now. See what you think.

"Good morning. My name is Dee Blick from The Marketing Gym Ltd. I am an award-winning Chartered Marketer and I work with many local businesses like yours, improving their profitability through powerful marketing on a shoestring budget. Do you have a few moments now to talk about what you look for from your marketing and how I could benefit your business?"

Let's take a closer look at this introduction. It is very simple and it takes about 15 seconds to deliver.

o It's important to give your full name and your business name. You sound professional and this distances you from the telesales introduction.

o If you have won any awards or accreditations, include these within your opening few lines. They establish credibility quickly and you may well be quizzed on the detail further into the conversation.

o What's the big benefit that you deliver? Communicate this within those opening lines. Are you local? Have you achieved some fantastic results with other similar companies? Do you specialise in this particular sector?

o If you want to develop a positive two-way conversation then you must ask for permission to talk. If they agree to the conversation you can proceed with confidence and without worrying that they could end the call at any moment. What if they tell you that now is not a good time? Ask them when would be a more convenient time to call. Put the date and time in your diary and be sure to follow up.

It will help if you spend a little time mapping out your introduction. Ideally, don't go beyond 30 seconds and practice what you want to say until it becomes second nature.

How to Handle Those Initial Objections

In an ideal world, after your introduction it should be all systems go. Unfortunately, in the real world you can find yourself on the receiving end of objections within moments of making your introduction. Here are three common objections that you may encounter and how you can respond to them in a professional and positive manner.

1.   "We already have a supplier who does this for us."

"That's a good reason why we should talk. Many of our existing clients were with another provider and by moving to us they…" (Discuss the key benefits your clients gained from the switch - greater value, better level of service, more local service, higher specification of product and so on)

Or your answer could be:

"That's a good reason why we should talk. Many of our existing clients use more than one supplier and we're not looking to move you away from your supplier. At this stage I am keen to find out how we can add value to your business with our services."

2.   "We don't really use (your products or services) here."

"Could I ask out of curiosity, if you don't use our services how do you…?" (Add here what you believe is their need)

3.   "We don't use (your products or services) because they're too expensive."

"I can understand why you would say that because it's a comment that some of our existing clients made before they understood what we really do offer and how we add value through…" (Add here your big benefit)

Or your answer could be:

"Can I just ask in relation to what? I know that our existing clients use us because of the value that we deliver. But I can understand that

if you haven't worked with us before you may think that we're too expensive and it would be useful to know why you think that is the case."

Don't be defensive when you are met with objections. Show that you understand their concern and that they're not the only person to have raised this particular objection. Then try to end with a positive message about your business. This should not be a confrontation. Winning a war of words is no consolation for the loss of the potential new business.

It pays to handle objections calmly, with confidence and without irritation. The fact that the person is raising reasonable objections suggests that they are genuinely interested in finding out more about you. Sometimes when the person that you're speaking to makes a challenging statement, it's a good idea to make a note of it and come back to it later in the conversation.

Building Rapport - Asking Questions

How much does that person really need your products or services? Unless you are asking the questions that will determine this, you can get carried away with the sound of your own voice. At the end of the call you could realise that you actually know very little about the person. By asking questions, you are sending out a clear message that you're interested in what that person has to say, rather than in what you have to say.

So, what are the fact-finding questions that you should be asking a person in the first cold call? It's a good idea to write down the key questions to which you must have answers before you can even consider suggesting a meeting. Try not to exceed three or four questions. Any more and you risk sounding like an interrogator.

Once the conversation is in full flow, you will find yourself asking and responding to questions quite naturally.

In my experience, it's always a good idea to explain why you are asking a particular question.

*"Could I ask how you currently market your business **so that** I can understand the challenges that you are facing?"*

*" Can I start by asking what you believe is the biggest challenge that you face with your computer network **so that** I can understand whether our company can offer any solutions?"*

*"Can I ask how many people are in your team **so that** I can identify exactly how our training services can benefit you?"*

For every single question where your aim is to gather information so that you can build up an understanding of genuine need, you will get a much better response if you explain to the person why you are asking it.

Textbooks are full of advice about open questions and closed questions and how they should be used during a conversation. Don't become hung up on whether you have just asked a closed question instead of an open question and so on. You're trying to build a positive and mutually beneficial dialogue so focus on doing just that. Concentrating on too many rules can hinder your natural communication skills.

To help you, here are the four questions that I try to ask in a conversation. They help me to understand the level of interest that the person has in the products or services that I'm discussing, and the budget available to them. They also help keep the conversation flowing nicely without awkward pauses. You might find them useful also I hope.

- o If you could change just one thing about (the product or service we are discussing) what would that be?

- o Can I ask whether you allocate a budget for (the product or service we are discussing)

- o We would really like to do business with you. Why aren't we?

- o What are your thoughts on our discussions so far?

Start to think about the range of questions that you really need to ask a cold prospect. Make a list of them and talk them through before you pick up the telephone. Keep them close at hand so that you can glance at them periodically if necessary.

Building Rapport – Listening

It's tempting when you're passionate about your product or service to talk to the extent that there is no time for feedback. Rather than building a two-way conversation, you are in fact engaging in a spot of public speaking on the telephone. It's time to stop talking and start listening. Demonstrate that you are listening in the following ways:

- **When you ask a question, allow the person to answer** you without interruption. When they have finished speaking, allow a few seconds to elapse before you start talking again.

- **Don't interrupt the person** even if you have something relevant to say. Make a note and refer back to it later in the conversation.

- **Let the person know that you are listening** by quietly murmuring 'yes' whilst they are talking. If you listen in complete silence, with no form of acknowledgement, they will start to worry that you are not listening to them or that you are bored.

- **Summarise some of the key** points that the person has made, especially the really positive ones! This will also ensure that there is no misunderstanding.

- **Seek clarification** of what has been said in a positive way. "So can I just confirm?"

It's natural to want to interrupt when you know that you have something really interesting to contribute to the conversation. In a face-to-face situation, you can often get away with this but the telephone is not so forgiving. In your early days of telephone cold calling, try to focus on listening to what is being said to you, without interrupting. You will find it challenging at times, but it is worth persevering with. It shows that you are interested, professional and respectful. In short, it shows that you are not a telesales executive.

Building Rapport - Paying Genuine Compliments

There's nothing worse than a person paying you a compliment that is obviously insincere because they want to seal the deal. You can see right through it. However, paying genuine compliments that are relevant to the telephone conversation can have a very positive effect. The secret lies in not overdoing it.

Here are a few compliments that can be effective on the telephone and that I use. Put them into words that you feel comfortable using, but try to keep the meaning behind them. Make sure that you are sincere and that the compliment is appropriate to your conversation.

- o "Thank you for your time, I have really enjoyed our conversation."

- o "I really appreciate the time you have given me as I know you're busy."

- o "You sound as though you really enjoy your job."

- o "I've learnt a lot from you in a short space of time, thank you."

- o "You have been so helpful, thank you."

- o "You sound as though you have a very successful business."

- o "I really appreciate your honesty in sharing this information with me."

- o "Thank you for your positive feedback on our products and services."

- o "You are obviously very successful at what you do."

Aim to make the person that you have called feel pleased that they downed their tools to listen to what you had to say.

Building Up To a Positive Finish

Ending the call is one of the most important parts of your telephone conversation. It's the time when you need to bring a positive conversation to a positive end or to bid farewell to those calls where you know that there's little point continuing.

Here are some suggestions for ending a call successfully:

- **Book in a follow-up call if you are sending** something in the meantime. If the person wants to find out more about you and has requested that you put something in the post or that you provide contact details of one of your clients as a reference, make sure that you arrange a follow-up call to discuss their thoughts. Aside from the fact that you want to take the relationship to the next stage, there are practical reasons for a follow up process. When you are calling back, you can glide effortlessly past any type of gatekeeper because your call is no longer cold. When booking in a follow-up call, actually book a specific date and an approximate time in the diary rather than just saying "I will call you in a few weeks time." That way, there's more chance of the person being available to take your call.

- **Go for a meeting if all the signs are positive.** If the initial call has gone well, it would be akin to wasting a fantastic opportunity not to suggest a meeting. Explain why you are suggesting a meeting. You believe that on the basis of your conversation your products and services are going to be of real benefit to this business. Suggest a date and let the person know that they can find out more from your website. Make sure that you confirm the details of the meeting within a few minutes of the call ending via e-mail.

- **Don't shy away from requesting a meeting** because you fear rejection. If all the signs are good, suggest a meeting with confidence. If you are met with reluctance, empathise with their decision – the option of a meeting will be there after they have read a little more about you or after they have spoken to one of your clients as a reference.

- **Be prepared to remind your prospect** who you are again when you do make that follow-up call. Unless they have an immediate need for your services the chances are that they will have placed you on their 'back burner'. This is natural so don't take any forgetfulness personally. Don't be surprised either if your information is still sitting in their pending tray. Although arranging another telephone call is a safe option, try suggesting an informal meeting to save your contact from going through your information. *Just because they said no to a meeting in the first phone call, doesn't mean they will say no this time.* Their circumstances may have changed and you could be calling at a very good time. If you don't ask you won't know. I have arranged many meetings that have led to business opportunities using this approach.

- **Find another word instead of 'meeting'** if you're talking to a very busy person. Suggest 'an informal chat' or taking 'a brief window of your time.' or suggest getting together for 30 minutes before they start work or maybe after work. Don't assume that because they can't give you much time that they're not interested in your products or services. I can remember arranging a meeting with the sales director of a large insurance broker one morning and although I had initially suggested 30 minutes, on the day itself the meeting lasted 90 minutes. When you actually get in front of people, you usually find that they are willing to give you more of their time than was initially agreed.

- **Be patient.** It may take several calls to get anywhere. One of my biggest cold call achievements was to secure Direct Line as a client yet they rejected the idea of a meeting several times. 'No' can often mean 'Not now'. Unless your intuition tells you that you're not getting anywhere, then it's worth persevering and taking things slowly.

- **Don't leave the small details to memory.** It's natural to get carried away during a positive telephone conversation and only when you put the receiver down, do you realise that you've forgotten to take some essential details. Make sure that you gather as much of the following information as possible and write it down:

  o Confirmation of name, job title, salutation. Are you confident that you have the correct spelling? No one appreciates follow-up mailings and e-mails with the wrong details.

  o Confirmation of e-mail address so that you can communicate by e-mail in between telephone calls and mailings.

  o If a meeting has been arranged in a few weeks time, tell your prospect that you will call a few days beforehand to confirm that arrangements are still convenient. There is nothing more frustrating than turning up to a meeting and your prospect has forgotten all about it.

o When you have arranged a meeting, it's a good idea to confirm its planned duration, whether there is a parking space available or a nearby car park and how many people will be attending. It can be a bit disconcerting to turn up expecting to present to one person and find half a dozen people in the boardroom staring back at you!

o Make sure that you follow-up on any promises. If you have promised to send information, do so. If a person in your organisation needs to make the follow-up call, brief them thoroughly and check that they make that call. If you have provided details of some of your clients as references, brief your clients on what to expect when the call comes through.

Tips for when Using a Telemarketing Business to Make Your Cold Calls

It may be that although you are going to give telephone cold calling your very best shot, you are open to the idea at some stage of using a telemarketing company to make cold calls on your behalf. If you are, then it pays to ask plenty of questions before you part with your hard earned cash. Jacky Misson is the Director of the business-to-business Telemarketing Company, Nido Marketing. Here, she gives an insight into what you should be looking out for together with the key questions that you should be asking any telemarketing company before you seal the deal. Use them as the basis for your fact-finding.

- **Do your research on the Web and** draw up a shortlist of telemarketing companies you want to speak to. Generally speaking, a call centre is suitable for promoting low value products with an emphasis on generating a high volume of daily calls. A niche telemarketing company is much more suited to campaigns where decision-makers are being targeted with high-value products or services and the emphasis is on generating intelligent conversations and meetings.

- **How do they sound on the phone** when you call to enquire about their telemarketing services? The way they respond to you and how they handle your enquiry is a good indication of how they will represent your company.

- **What are their premises like?** Light and airy or dark and dingy? People tend to perform better in a healthy and welcoming environment especially when they can be on the telephone for most of the day.

- **How helpful and friendly are the people** you are meeting and the rest of the team for that matter?

- **What is their staff retention rate?** Do people come and go or do they stay and regard this as a career? Happy, stable teams deliver the best results for your business.

- **Do they show a clear understanding** of your needs or are they just saying what they want you to hear?

- **What questions are they asking about your data?** They should be able to clean or augment your data and source new leads from reputable data houses if required.

- **Be wary if they make guarantees about results.** It is difficult to predict the outcome of any telemarketing campaign before the campaign has actually begun. However, ask if they have any experience in your sector.

- **Make sure that you meet the people** who will be making calls on your behalf. They will become the custodians of your brand.

- **What systems do they use to record** the outcomes of conversations they have had with your cold prospects? How frequently will they be feeding this information back to you and who will be feeding back - a manager removed from the day-to-day calling or one of the actual calling team?

- **How many people will be working** on your campaign? Ideally, they should be the same people over a period of time.

- **Are they able to gather** useful market intelligence at the same time as making your calls?

- **How flexible and adaptable** are they to change goals and targets part way through a campaign if needed?

Finally, always trust your gut instinct and ask if you can speak to existing clients before making your final decision.

Measure Your Success on a Regular Basis

If you persevere with cold calling then you will start to get results. However keep in mind that rejections are an inevitable part of your journey to success. Every month ensure that you review your telephone cold calling activity and the impact that it is having on your sales.

- o How many introductory cold calls have you made?
- o How many follow-up calls have you made?

   o How many meetings have you arranged?

   o What sales are in the pipeline?

   o How many sales have you actually completed?

   o What percentage of your total sales does the telephone contribute?

These questions will help you measure how effective your telephone cold calling has been. It's also a good idea to review what you are saying on the telephone and where you need to make improvements or changes. Keep your benefits relevant and up-to-date and if your market conditions change, consider changing your message.

Finally, if you find that telephone cold calling is your main route to success, don't be afraid to increase the amount of time that you are spending on it. And make sure that you celebrate every single meeting and every single sale because you will have worked really hard to get those results!

4 POWERFUL TARGETED DIRECT MAIL

Direct mail has often been on the receiving end of negative press and not without good reason. Thousands of direct mail communications are sent to consumers and business people alike every year, and in many cases the content is of no interest whatsoever. But there's another side to this story, which is that targeted direct mail is potentially an extremely powerful and effective form of marketing. And for a small business in particular, direct mail can yield exciting results. Let me explain a little more about this.

For the first 10 years of my marketing career, I was responsible for planning and implementing the annual direct mail programmes for one of the biggest insurance companies in the UK. When I began to work with small businesses, I realised that the techniques, tools and tricks that I had learnt in the previous years, could be applied successfully to smaller direct mail campaigns with equally good results. In fact I continue to be amazed by the results that a small business can get from a simple mailshot sent to just 20 people. So in this chapter we are going to look at how you can develop effective and targeted direct mail campaigns to engage clients and cold prospects alike. We are not looking at sending thousands of random direct mail communications (that can have the effect of draining your budget and your enthusiasm). We will focus our energies instead on how you can send small and targeted mailshots. This means looking at the following:

- The benefits of direct mail for a small business
- The common mistakes to avoid

- Who do you want to mail?
- Mailing lists - what you need to know
- Why do you want to mail?
- Your call to action and the Continuum of Behaviour
- Deciding upon what to mail
- Lumpy mail!
- How many people should you mail?
- To follow up or not
- What responses can you expect?
- Measuring the impact

The Benefits of Direct Mail for a Small Business

Direct mail has many advantages for a small business, and here are a few of them:

- **It is a really cost-effective way to reach** both prospects and existing clients. The cost can amount to no more than stationery and stamps.

- **It's a good way to encourage the recipient** of your mailshot to act, whether you want them to pick up the phone and contact you, visit your website or to be in the right frame of mind when you contact them.

- **It's an easy method of keeping in touch**. You can make the decision to communicate relevant and interesting news about your business or products and services, and within one or two days your mailshot is on the doormat.

- **It can help to build and reinforce your brand**. A well-crafted and targeted letter plus an attractive piece of promotional material, can really grab attention if sent to a targeted recipient.

- **You can use direct mail to bring your products** and services to life with samples, case studies and special offers etc.

- **It is also a way to generate leads.** Direct mail on its own can sometimes create so much interest in a prospect that you are being contacted, before you have picked up the phone to follow-up the mailshot.

- **You can accurately target** with whom you want to communicate, right down to the individual person. You can also decide when you want to communicate with them.

- **You can measure and test** the impact of your mailshot. You often know within a matter of days whether a mailshot has worked and by continually testing and refining your approach, you can increase the responses from future campaigns.

In the rest of the chapter, we will consider how to increase your sales with small-targeted direct mail campaigns, but not before we have looked at some of the direct mail mistakes that a small business owner can make.

The Common Mistakes to Avoid

Many small businesses embark on direct mail campaigns and become frustrated. Responses are low and little if any business is generated. Here are some of the reasons why their direct mail campaigns may have fallen short in delivering the results they hoped for.

- **They haven't really thought about** why they are using direct mail as a communication tool. This general lack of clarity comes through in the content of the mailshot itself.

- **They lack the experience and knowledge** of what works and what doesn't work with direct mail. This general lack of awareness can be the difference between a campaign failing miserably and being a spectacular success.

- **There has been no prior testing of a mailing list.** Everyone is mailed and the results can be either mediocre or disastrous. The cost of what turned out to be a futile exercise can discourage a small-business owner from ever using direct mail as a marketing tool again.

- **Poor quality data**. A large proportion of the detail held on each person is either incorrect or incomplete. This can result in many unopened mailshots being returned, often with irate messages scribbled on the envelope.

- **The contents of the mailshot are drab and boring.** The letter has no purpose or call to action, is littered with spelling mistakes and it looks unprofessional. Any accompanying enclosures are also prone to falling into the same trap.

You don't want to make these mistakes. Every single piece of direct mail that you send should be relevant, engaging and above all, targeted. You don't want to mail everybody, you only want to mail people that you believe have an interest in what you have to offer. It is not that difficult to get good responses from your mailshots. You are looking at an investment of your time and of course your creativity. But before we get creative, let's firstly turn our attention to identifying who is going to receive your mailshots.

Who Do You Want to Mail?

Okay, you're interested in using direct mail as a communication tool. The next stage is deciding who you want to target. Let's consider some of the groups you could be looking at:

o   Your existing clients.

o   Warm prospects -potential clients that you have been in contact with, but are yet to do business with.

o   Lapsed clients -previous clients that are no longer doing business with you but with whom you would like to maintain contact in the hope of winning their business back.

o   Cold prospects - potential clients that you have previously identified. You have their contact details but nothing more.

o   The target audiences you have defined in your marketing plan. You've done your research on each group and you know why you want to target them, but you have not gone any further as yet.

Time for a spot of spring-cleaning!

At this stage, it's useful if you can spend time planning in detail the different groups that you would like to target.

Identify the numbers in each of your groups of clients, warm prospects and lapsed clients. You may only have a handful of names if you are a new business. On the other hand, you may have hundreds or more. Time now to look at the accuracy of the information that you have gathered. Don't think that it doesn't matter if some of the details that you have on your files are incorrect. Validating the records that you hold to ensure they are still up-to-date is a very important task. As we identified earlier, one of the reasons why so many direct mail communications end up in the bin, is because the details of the person receiving the mail are incorrect. You know yourself how unlikely you are to open an envelope if your surname or the name of your business is incorrect. At the very heart of all successful direct mail campaigns is accurate and reliable data. This applies whether you are using your own data or mailing names and addresses from a list that you have rented or bought. If you don't have enough time to clean your data, get someone to do this for you. It won't take long and it will be an extremely useful exercise. The most efficient way of doing this is by telephone.

How easy is it to access your data?

I work with many small businesses where they only hold basic client records, often linked to the accounting system. They may have the details of their cold prospects on a spreadsheet or in paper-based files. Lapsed clients are sometimes buried in their system. With so many different sources of data scattered about in different locations, it can be challenging, (although not impossible) to plan direct mail campaigns. At the other end of the scale, others have a very sophisticated system in which they can identify the names and addresses for mailing in seconds, whether they are lapsed clients, cold prospects or existing clients. Then, as responses start coming in, they are able to update each record with the results. If your data is spread across a number of paper based and computer files, you may want to consider investing in a contact management system designed with the needs of a small business in mind. Before you begin your investigations, find out if your existing system can be upgraded. One client had a very basic system where his current client records were linked to his accounting system and cold prospects and lapsed clients were located on a separate system altogether. Thankfully, all it took was for a friendly and helpful IT expert to make the necessary changes for all the data to be in one simple system. This solution was put in place for less than the cost of buying an off-the-shelf solution. If you decide to invest in a contact management system, ask for a free trial and quiz other small businesses about the systems they use. The most popular one that I have come across and that many clients use is ACT, but do some research yourself and you may find other systems that you prefer.

Mailing Lists - What You Need to Know

If you want to target cold prospects but you currently have no specific names, you're going to have to locate them. One of the easiest ways to locate cold prospects is by renting or buying a mailing list. In my experience, this is an area where a small business owner can spend hundreds or thousands of pounds and still not end up with the names they were looking to target in the first place.

There are many organisations that sell or rent mailing lists. Data-base marketing companies specialise in offering either consumer lists or business-to-business lists. They are usually either licensees of an extensive database, or they own lists that they have compiled themselves. When you are researching mailing lists, you will also come across list brokers. They also offer lists to buy or rent, where the information that has gone into compiling each list will have been derived from many different sources. A little further on, we are going to look at the types of questions that you should be asking before parting with any money. But let's look at an alternative to the traditional mailing lists, and one that may be more suited to your business. Thomson Directories have a system called Business Search PRO that is extremely popular with small businesses (*www.businesssearch.com*). It is an online directory of business names that can be easily manipulated to meet the requirements of your business as follows:

o It holds the details of over 2 million businesses. If you are looking to target other businesses, it is therefore likely that you will find them.

o You can take advantage of a free 24-hour trial that gives sufficient time to explore how the system works and of course to search for the businesses that you want to locate before making any decision to buy.

o The data is updated weekly, and cleaned on a monthly basis to ensure that any business subscribing to the Telephone Preference Services is removed.

o You pay an annual fee to access the system and make your searches. The search facility is fantastic and can be as wide or as narrow as you want to make it. If you want to find out for example how many hairdressers are in your town, you can access this information in seconds and find other useful information such as the number of employees and contact details.

o One of the biggest benefits of Business Search PRO is that it's ideal for small, targeted direct mailings because you don't have to download a minimum number of records. If you are planning to send out just 5 or 10 mailshots each week to cold prospects, you simply download 5 or 10 records. This compares favourably to mailing lists where the numbers that you have to buy or rent can run into thousands of names and whether you want that amount or not, you still have to pay for it.

However, don't dismiss the idea of renting or buying a mailing list. For larger mailings they can still be very useful. But bear in mind that if you're planning to send out only a small number of targeted direct mailshots, a list of thousands of names is not really appropriate. It's a better idea to buy the data that you need, in small quantities. Any list will start to age from the moment you receive it, so don't buy any data until you need it.

What should you be asking a list owner?

Before you make any decisions about buying or renting a mailing list, it's a good idea to do some background research. You don't want to end up with a list that has cost you money to buy and yet includes a large proportion of incorrect data. The resulting mailshots will consequently be poorly targeted and the whole exercise will be destined to fail. A reputable list owner or list broker will usually be a member of The List Warranty Register. If they are members, The List Warranty Register logo will be on their website and company literature. The Register is committed to promoting best practice in the list industry and the Warranty is your assurance that the data has been collected lawfully, is up-to-date and complies with relevant codes of practice. If you want to find out more, visit *www.dma.org.uk* the website of the Direct Marketing Association. I personally use a company called Marketscan, (*www.marketscan.co.uk*) because they are members of the Direct Marketing Association and The List Warranty Register. Their website also allows you to search for your data before making enquiries about costs.

Here are the questions I ask a list owner when I'm interested in renting or buying a list from them (I also make sure that I get their answers in writing). I hope that you find these questions useful too.

- **What size is the list?** Can you rent or buy a portion of it? What are the minimum numbers that can be selected? Is there a minimum charge?

- **What sources of information have been used** to gather and compile the data? Has it been verified for accuracy and if so, has a person picked up the phone and confirmed with everyone on the list that their details are correct?

- **How old is the list?** If the answer is a few years old, you should enquire how the list owner keeps the data accurate and up to date. A good list will be cleaned regularly as discussed earlier. Some lists are only cleaned on a reactive basis meaning that individual records are only removed or changed when the list owner is alerted to the change of details by a scribbled message on a returned envelope. It's not a good idea to rent or buy a list that is cleaned in such an ad hoc manner because the likelihood is that a fair amount of the data will be incorrect.

- **The data that is held for each contact** on the list should include the full name of a contact including their salutation, a business name, address, a postcode and a telephone number. You should be looking for this amount of information as a bare minimum.

- **If you rent the list, can you only use it once?** Don't assume that renting a list gives you the automatic right to use it as many times as you want. You usually have to specify how many times you are planning to use it and are charged accordingly. With most rented lists, the list owner will add 'seed names' so that they can check on any unauthorised use of their list. If you've only paid to use a list once, and you decide to use it again, you could find yourself with an unexpected bill.

- **How will the list be supplied to you?** Usually, it will be in the form of a spreadsheet, but it's always worth checking beforehand.

- **By now, the list owner will either be delighted** that you are so well-informed with all your questions or they will be rather nervous! Bring your questions to a conclusion by asking whether they clean their list each month so that it complies with the many preference services, including the Telephone Preference Service and the Corporate Telephone Preference Service (more information on this in chapter 3). If you're planning on following up some of the people you have mailed with a telephone call, you don't want to be contacting people that have subscribed to these services.

When you are satisfied with the answers you have been given and you are equally satisfied that the names on the list represent the people you want to communicate with, you can make your decision to rent or buy the list with confidence. Referring back to the point made earlier about getting the answers in writing, it's important to do this because if the list turns out to be less than satisfactory, you are in a strong position to negotiate for a refund. Bear in mind also that if you do buy a list this doesn't give you the sole rights to use it. The list owner will continue to sell or rent the list to other people. Buying a list simply means you are not under any restrictions on how frequently you use it. But remember, data does start to age from the moment it is purchased, so don't buy or rent a list until you are actually planning on using it.

Why Do You Want to Mail?

Earlier on, we outlined some of the benefits of direct mail for a small business. The reason why most small businesses use direct mail as a communication tool is because they want to sell more products and services and direct mail is a very useful stepping-stone on this path. Start by understanding whether direct mail is appropriate for your business. For example, some of the reasons for mailing may be:

o You're planning to use direct mail to build awareness of your business and your brand. You want to be more visible with the people that are in the market for your products and services.

o You want to fill the gap in between telephone calls and your other marketing activities such as networking and PR.

o You want to introduce your business by showcasing what you do to people that have not heard from you before.

o You want to promote a specific product in your range, or a brand new service that you are now offering.

o To generate warm leads so that you can progress to a face-to-face meeting.

o Your brand new website is up and running. You want people to visit it, sign up for your newsletter, read your blog, and view your online catalogue.

o You want to build awareness of your products and services over a period of time by using a programme of regular mailshots.

It's likely that you will have a combination of reasons for wanting to use direct mail, rather than just one on its own. For example you may want to introduce your business to people that don't know about you, yet at the same time you would like also to promote your new website. Your reasons will also vary depending upon whom you are mailing. With existing clients, your reasons for mailing will differ from your reasons for mailing cold prospects. Existing clients already know what you do and most of them will be loyal to you. Cold prospects that have never heard from you before have no such loyalty. With every single mailshot you are planning to send out you need to align your reasons for sending it with your relationship with the recipient.

Your Call to Action and the Continuum of Behaviour

Regardless of who is receiving your mailshot there are two important things to consider when creating it.

- **You must include a rallying cry,** otherwise known as a call to action. This is where you direct the recipient to do something that will be of benefit to them and your business.

- **You need to ensure that what you're asking** a person to do is both realistic and appropriate given the nature of your message and the relationship that you have with them. We have touched on this in the previous section, but will now cover it in more detail.

First of all, what do we mean by a rallying cry or a call to action? Within most successful direct mailers, is a message designed to motivate the recipient to act. Typically, it can go along the lines of:

- o Please contact us for a quotation
- o Please contact us for an initial chat to explore your needs
- o Please visit our website and sign up to our newsletter
- o Please contact us to arrange a free trial
- o Please complete our survey

Naturally, with your own business, you will develop an appropriate call to action. The general principle behind it is to encourage a progression in the relationship. Start to think what you want your call to action to be. It will vary depending upon the people you are mailing and what is being promoted. This possibly means establishing a different call to action for each mailshot that you send out. You must also take into consideration the need to make your call to action both realistic and appropriate. I use a tried and tested marketing tool to help me with this. It is called the 'Continuum of Behaviour'. It is built around the decision-making process that a person follows before deciding whether to do business with you. There are five stages to this process:

- o Awareness
- o Interest
- o Evaluation
- o Desire
- o Action

The Continuum of Behaviour reflects the stages of progression in a relationship where different decisions are made at different stages.
Let's look at this tool in more detail using a couple of examples. First of all we will consider cold prospects that know nothing about your business, and then move on to look at existing clients.

Before you can sell your products and services to cold prospects, they have to be aware you exist. Having made them aware of your presence, you build upon this by generating their interest in what you have to offer. If you are going to use direct mail to introduce yourself to a cold prospect, then the purpose of your initial mailer should be to generate awareness of your business. If you try and get them to sign up within just one communication, you are likely to be unsuccessful because you are asking for too much given the lack of any relationship. Your call to action should instead centre on encouraging your cold prospect to find out even more about what you do.

Now, let's take a look at seeking new business from your existing clients. Because they know you, are loyal to you and have bought from you before, it's likely that your reasons for using direct mail to communicate with them will differ from your reasons for mailing cold prospects. You don't need to build any awareness of your business and your clients are already interested in using you. Therefore, including words to describe your business and what you do is unnecessary, whereas this is vital with cold prospects. Your call to action with your existing clients can be more direct. You can, for example, encourage existing clients to contact you to arrange a meeting (provided this is what you want your mailing to achieve). Referring back to the Continuum of Behaviour, you are aiming to move beyond the stages of awareness, interest and evaluation into desire. If clients want to meet with you, it will then be up to you at the meeting to move your clients to the final stage on the Continuum, action!

When you really get into the swing of direct mail, it's possible that you will have several mailing campaigns on the go at any one time with each one aimed at a different group as outlined earlier. For every single group, you need to look at the mailing you are planning to send and ensure that both your reasons for mailing and your call to action are realistic. Use the Continuum of Behaviour to identify where the people you are mailing are currently placed. Are they aware of you? Are they sufficiently interested in what you offer? Are they in a position to evaluate your products and services? Do they have a strong desire to do business with you?

Generate the right message and the right call to action and you are on your way towards achieving some great results. This thoughtful and considered approach to direct mail is at the opposite end of the spectrum to the dreaded junk mail approach. You are not mailing people with a confused message combined with an unrealistic call to action. Instead you are creating relevant and targeted messages with calls to action that reflect the nature of the relationship.

Deciding Upon What to Mail

You are now at the stage where you know who you want to mail. You've spent time looking at why you want to mail and what your call to action is going to be each time. Time now to decide what you are actually going to include in your mailshot. It's at this stage you can be tempted to part with large sums of money by creating glossy brochures, catalogues and sales presentations. I would not recommend this. Not only are you at risk of spending money on which you are unlikely to see significant return, you don't usually need to go to these lengths to create a mailshot that gets results. You can achieve excellent results using shoestring principles without opting for a "cheap and cheerful" approach. A word of warning, however. You can go to the other extreme and spend money on poor quality flyers as the basis of your direct mail communications. The result when you take this approach is that your mailshot usually flies very quickly from the doormat to the bin. We are therefore going to look at two effective and simple communications - the sales letter and the newsletter.

The sales letter

This is often conspicuous by its absence. You open the envelope addressed to you personally, and inside are a few sales flyers and nothing more. To find out who has sent this information you have to search in vain for a contact name. You're not impressed. If they had gone to the trouble of including a letter that explained what was being offered, they may have been in with a shout of at least getting your interest. Instead, they are pinning their hopes on a few random sales flyers, probably mailed out to thousands of people with no thought about targeting.

At the heart of a good mailshot is a letter. It communicates the purpose of your mailing, and how the recipient can benefit from this information. The good news is that it costs you very little to create a great sales letter. You simply need decent quality letterhead paper, a printer that is up to the job and some flair. But before you start writing your letter, it is important that you revisit your reasons for sending out this mailshot and look at who will be receiving it. You need to write your letter with this thought firmly in your mind so that your content is both relevant and targeted. You can then use these tips to guide you.

- **Generally speaking, a great sales letter** is one that communicates a message simply, clearly and with passion. If you can communicate using everyday words and phrases, you are working on the right lines. Don't be afraid to write as you would talk. You are not creating a technical bulletin; you are composing a friendly and enthusiastic letter. Make sure to use the word "you" throughout rather than continually referring to "I", and aim for bite sized chunks of text rather than one big block. Use bullet points to reinforce your key messages and if you're communicating something of real importance, embolden it.

- **How long should your letter be?** In theory you can take as long as it needs to communicate your message. However,

I would recommend that you limit your initial letters to one side of A4. You can always write longer letters as your confidence improves.

- **What about the content itself?** You only have a few seconds before the recipient of your letter will make the decision either to continue reading or head for the bin. You may have a little longer with an existing client, but with a cold prospect you don't have that luxury. You must grab the attention within the opening lines of your letter. In terms of structure you can open up your letter with an introductory paragraph, or you can open it up with a headline that you embolden, followed by a paragraph of text. In those opening few lines, you need to focus upon the central message of your letter and why the reader should be interested in finding out more. What are you offering that will make a significant change or improvement to this person's business or life?

- **How are you going to reinforce** this attention-grabbing introduction? You're now moving into the middle part of your letter. If you have plenty to say, use short paragraphs and embolden the first three or four words of each paragraph. This will make your letter easier to read and it helps the reader to focus on the key messages. Can you share a customer testimonial, or outline a positive case study that will further substantiate your message? Can you share some interesting facts and statistics on what you are promoting, for example *"In just one day we guarantee to turn you into an accomplished public speaker. We currently have 100% customer satisfaction."*

- **In the final part of your letter**, your closing paragraph should be looking to reinforce and summarise the key benefits. Include any offers and in the last few lines sign off with your call to action-what you would like the recipient to do next.

- **Don't be happy to settle on your first draft.** Spend some time reviewing it. Are you sure there are no spelling mistakes or poor grammar? Is the message clear and well written? It's likely that it will take a few attempts before you have a sales letter that you are willing to show your colleagues and maybe even a few clients. Tell them who the letter is aimed at and ask for honest feedback.

- **The devil is in the detail!** When you have the final version of your letter make sure that you hand sign each one. On one campaign that I was responsible for, we managed to double the responses simply by ensuring that the Managing Director personally signed each letter. The letter that had been sent out in the previous campaign was exactly the same but without his signature. Paying attention to small details like this can make the difference between your letter being read and acted upon, and landing in the bin.

- **When sending your letter to a cold prospect**, always attach your business card. Not only does your mailshot look more professional, it can in my experience, actually increase your responses. If, despite your very best efforts, your letter is disregarded, your business card could still find its way into a business card holder and a few weeks or months down the line, you may be pleasantly surprised with a phone call.

Example sales letter: Eden HR Consulting

Eve Clennell is the Managing Director of Eden HR Consulting. Eve has grown her business primarily through networking and word-of-mouth recommendations but identified direct mail as the tool to enable her to reach cold prospects. Local businesses in the hospitality sector were identified for direct mailing. This is the letter that was sent to each contact, accompanied by Eve's business card and a professionally designed four-page newsletter. The reason why I have included this letter is because it demonstrates many of these tips in practice.

Dear Mrs Bloggs,

If HR is on your to-do list then Eden HR Consulting can be your powerful HR ally. We work with many organisations in the hospitality sector where clients say it's our hands-on approach to HR that is so invaluable in helping them cut through the maze of red tape that accompanies the recruitment, employment and redundancy process.

Do you have a pressing HR issue right now? Contracts of employment need updating… a member of staff is on long term sick and you're not sure how the law stands on this matter? You could be facing the prospect of taking an employee through a disciplinary and grievance process and you want to act fairly and within the law. Your staff handbook may be out of date but knowing how to bring it up to date to reflect the current age, disability and retirement legislation is a huge task.

Like many of our hospitality clients, your business may have reached the stage where HR guidance and advice is important but when to start and how to start is another matter altogether. Help is at hand!

You could benefit from an incredibly useful service that we currently offer to two organisations each month. Our "Ask the HR Expert" session gives you the opportunity (on a one-to-one basis) to discuss your pressing HR questions with a Chartered HR professional. The session lasts 90 minutes and is confidential. Not only will you get the answers to your HR questions, you will also walk away with a tool kit of practical, effective and up to the minute HR advice, tailored to your organisation. **We can health check existing contracts and policies and advise on whether you are complying fully with employment law. You may also be eligible for substantial tax savings that you are not currently aware of.**

There is no charge for this session. It is a genuine, high-value service that enables us to demonstrate our HR expertise and our hands-on approach to HR.

If you would like to find out more about this session and how your organisation could benefit, you can either e-mail info@edenhrconsulting.com call 01403 734455 or fax 01403 734456. Please remember to include your full contact details and your company name.

We look forward to hearing from you,

Yours sincerely

Eve Clennell,
Managing Director

Start planning those sales letters because they have a vital role to play in generating responses to your mailshots. The second piece of low-cost literature that we are now going to look at is newsletters.

Newsletters

There's no doubt about it, a well-written, interesting, and accurately targeted newsletter can generate strong response when included as part of a mailshot. Newsletters are suitable for any type of business and cost very little to produce. This is the case even if you engage professionals, such as designers and copywriters. Newsletters allow you to communicate in a friendly and engaging manner with the people that you are doing business with, and the ones you are yet to do business with. A newsletter can promote your business for a modest cost when compared with a brochure or a content-limiting postcard or flyer. They help you to maintain contact with existing clients and warm prospects and to say a powerful hello to cold prospects. As with anything worth striving for, a great newsletter that delivers results takes time to plan and produce. Use these tips to get started.

- **Decide why you want a newsletter** beyond it simply being a useful communication tool for direct mail. Revisit your earlier reasons for mailing. These may include building a stronger awareness with both existing and new target clients, promoting your new or existing products, communicating your capabilities and using the law of attraction to show how well you are doing. A newsletter can be appropriate for each of these reasons.

- **Who are you aiming your newsletter at?** Go back to those target audiences outlined earlier. These are the people that will be receiving your newsletter and so as with writing your sales letter, you need to bear these people in mind when deciding on the content of your newsletter.

- **When do you plan to send it and how long** before you issue a new one? Timing is important and if, for example, you have an event or a launch coming up, you want to ensure that your newsletter hits those mats at the right time. You also need to look at those periods in the year when you need to be proactively generating business.

- **You may be brilliant at running your business,** but are you a great designer too? So many newsletters end up in the bin because they look homemade and unprofessional. Using the same principles outlined in Chapter 5, talk to a few designers and ask to see samples of their newsletters. Agree a fixed-price that should also include a PDF of the newsletter so that you can send it via e-mail or include it on the homepage of your website. If you're going to use images in your newsletter, a professional photographer is worth considering. Having a newsletter that people will admire and read is often worth paying a little extra for.

- **Similarly, if you're not confident in your creative** writing skills, then using an external copywriter can be a wise investment. Find a copywriter that demonstrates a good understanding of your business. Have they had previous experience of writing newsletters? Again, ask for a fixed fee. If you can do a spot of bartering, by offering your services in exchange for theirs, perhaps even better!

- **Content is king.** This is where you start to look at how you can create a compelling, easy to read and genuinely interesting newsletter, rather than a sales flyer. When that envelope is opened, you want your newsletter to jump out and inspire the reader. If you're stuck for content how about…

- **Including two or three testimonials** from happy clients. Don't overdo it. Two to three lines of text for each client should be enough to give a great impression.

- **A competition.** Ask two or three multiple-choice questions where the answers to each one can be found in the content of your newsletter. This is a really good way of ensuring your newsletter is read. Make sure that you offer a decent prize such as a bottle of champagne, a box of wine, an MP3 player or something of equal quality that is suitable for your brand. If you can also offer runner-up prizes, this will help to increase the response to your competition too. How about some goodie bags with nice promotional gifts, branded with your company details?

- **What have we been up to recently?** How about letting readers know the answer to this question with an interesting snapshot of approximately 200 words, giving an overview of any recent achievements and projects.

- **What do we do? It is always useful to include five or six** bullet points that outline what you do. Cold prospects will find this information useful and you may jog the memory of both existing and lapsed clients.

- **How about a guest writer?** Do you know someone who can write an interesting column in your newsletter? If so, consider offering them around 250 words. Ask them to discuss a topic that readers will find interesting. Top tips are always useful, and you can find out more about these in Chapter 7.

- **A short interview with you**… three to four questions that are geared to finding out what you enjoy about your business, what inspires you and what have been your biggest challenges to date.

- **An overview of your website.** If you have a cracking website, then promoting it in your newsletter with images of interesting pages and an overview of the contents is both helpful and interesting. It will also encourage people to visit your website.

- **A summary of your recent PR coverage.** You don't have to reproduce every column inch, but a summary of where you have been featured is enough to generate an interest in your business.

- **One or two client case studies.** Whether you are communicating to existing clients, warm leads or cold prospects, a few interesting client case studies can convey a really positive impression about your business. Aim for 150 to 200 words per case study and use the tips in Chapter 7 to help you.

At this stage, you will hopefully have plenty of ideas for your next newsletter. It is time now to think about the size.

You will need to decide whether to go for a two-sided A4 newsletter or a four-sided A4 newsletter. You can go smaller and opt for an A5 newsletter but if you do, make sure your newsletter runs to four sides because two sides will give the impression of a sales flyer.

Now, turn your attention to the word count. If you overfill your newsletter with text you will make it appear boring. Aim to write between 300 and 600 words on each page, depending on the balance you would like to strike between images and words. For example a photographer would probably aim for 300 words per page, as they would want to use most of the space to showcase their work. However, bear in mind that what is separating your newsletter from a sales flyer is that it's communicating interesting news and information about your business. Allow enough space for this.

When you use a newsletter as part of a mailshot, you are helping to build a valuable dialogue with the recipient. A truly great newsletter keeps you in the mind of your target audiences by showing your personality and your capabilities. It can tell clients and prospects about your business values and what you stand for, which is something that can't always be adequately described in more formal marketing communications. It also provides a reason for continued contact. Provided you have enough news about your business and the workload or cost is not prohibitive, you can create a number of newsletters each year.

Lumpy Mail!

I use the term "lumpy mail" to describe a mailshot where a gift is enclosed with the contents. The idea behind including a gift is that it puts the recipient in a positive frame of mind and encourages them to pay more attention to the contents than to a mailshot without a gift. This is not a new concept by any means and enclosing gifts within mailshots has been happening for decades. Some great results can be achieved if the gift is of a decent enough quality to actually create a positive impression. If it falls into the category of cheap and nasty, it will do more harm than good. Here are examples of how small businesses have used "lumpy mail."

Case study: TEK Express

TEK Express specialise in supporting the laptops and handheld devices of the mobile workforce of several large organisations. For many months, they had been trying to arrange meetings with 12 potential corporate clients they had identified as being suitable for their services. Arranging meetings by telephone had resulted in only a limited success and so a new approach was required and direct mail was chosen. A personal letter was created and sent to the relevant decision maker in each of the 12 companies. Accompanying the letter and business card was a high-quality pen that had been engraved with the initials of the decision maker. This had an amazing impact. Two of the recipients actually contacted TEK Express within a few days of the mailshot, and one of them, the National Blood Transfusion Service, agreed to a meeting. The final outcome was that TEK Express became a support agent for their laptops just four weeks after the postman had delivered the letter and the personalised pen.

Case study: Kalimex

Kalimex is a family-owned business that specialises in selling aftercare motor products through motor factors and car accessories shops. Each month Kalimex target their clients with newsletters, sales letters, sales tips and information bulletins. The message within each mailshot changes from month to month and this helps ensure interest levels are maintained. One month a client may be updated with Kalimex's PR coverage, in another month, a product will be promoted with a special offer attached. For the last few years, free gifts have been used to add some added sparkle to the monthly campaigns. These gifts include pens, drinks coasters, thermal drinks mugs filled with jellybeans and T-shirts. The ongoing feedback from Kalimex's clients to the gifts is extremely positive and this is reflected in the fact that four years down the line, responses show no signs of declining.

If you are keen to look at how promotional gifts can be used to increase the appeal of your mailshot these tips should help.

- **Set a budget so that you are not tempted** to overspend when you start looking for promotional gifts. For example, you can buy good-quality brand-name pens for under £1 each, including personalisation with your company details.

- **Decide how you're going to use your promotional gifts.** You may be looking at a number of different ways from enclosing them in your mailshots, using them as an incentive to encourage a response, or as a prize to a newsletter competition etc.

- **Make sure that the gifts you are considering** don't cost a fortune to post and no special packaging is needed to protect them from damage in transit.

- **Don't be tempted to use cheap throwaway gifts.** They will either create a bad impression or no impression at all. If you can find gifts that are attractive and environmentally friendly, better still. The humble pen is still one of the most popular gifts to send and receive, as are USB sticks and mugs. Aim for the best quality that you can achieve within your budget even if it means opting for lower quantities.

- **Don't be tempted into choosing gifts** that you really like unless you are targeting people that share your tastes. Think about what your target audiences would like and the environment in which they work. For example, if you are targeting people that work in an office environment, a gift they can use whilst at their desk would be useful. Branding your gifts with your company details is a good method of ensuring that your name is in front of them every day.

- **Always ask for a sample of any item** before deciding to buy. Ideally choose items that can be supplied in your corporate colours and that you believe are compatible with your brand and values.

How Many People Should You Mail?

The idea behind using targeted direct mail is that you can mail one or two people, or you can mail hundreds. When you start looking at mailing thousands of people, you have to be absolutely certain that you're going to get a response that fully justifies your costs, your time and energy. It's a much better idea to mail a smaller number as a test exercise before making the decision to mail thousands of people. If you can get into the habit of testing and then evaluating responses before launching into a much bigger mailing, you will increase your response rate. You will be able to gauge from the test mailing what works and what doesn't and use this information for the larger mailings. Mailing thousands of people with an untested mailshot can be an easy method of pouring money down the drain. Test, evaluate and roll out should be your three step approach. If you can start by making a weekly commitment to sending out say 10 or 20 targeted mailshots that is a much better approach than mailing 1000 prospects in one go and crossing your fingers. Get into the habit of sending out regular mailshots and you will find that the knowledge you gain each time will be invaluable. You'll soon arrive at the point where you have a very good idea of what it takes to create a winning format.

To Follow Up or Not

It's not always feasible, or necessary to follow up everyone on the mailshot list with a telephone call. However, you may want to think about creating categories of VIPs within your groups of cold prospects, warm prospects and existing and lapsed clients and call this select band three to five working days after they have received your mailshot. In all likelihood, this will lead to an increased response, but make sure that you keep a record of all responses so you can be sure that your additional effort is worthwhile.

Case study: Techmobility

Techmobility specialise in adapting vehicles for disabled motorists. Most of their customers are referred by the Motability specialists in car dealerships. Targeted monthly mailshots have played a key part in building their business. They are sent to existing clients and to cold prospects – those car dealerships that are yet to do business with Techmobility. Every mailshot has a different theme and message that is brought to life with newsletters, sales letters and information bulletins. Running in tandem with the direct mail programme is a targeted telemarketing programme in which 10 to 20 VIP cold prospects are identified and then called a few days after receiving the latest mailshot. This combination of a regular mailshot, and a personal follow-up telephone call has resulted in dozens of cold prospects becoming new clients. For existing clients, the monthly direct mailshots reinforce the value they gain from Techmobility.

What Responses Can You Expect?

It is almost impossible to predict the response that you will receive from any mailshots until you actually start sending out some test samples. By developing a practical understanding of what is successful and what is less so, you will see a pattern of responses emerge over time. This will help you to make an educated guess of likely responses to any planned mailshots. It is so important to test your initial ideas, and to be adopting the shoestring principles. The last thing that you want is to invest thousands of pounds in a mailshot that hasn't worked. If the biggest investment in a failed mailshot has been your time, it is not such a bitter pill to swallow.

In my experience, responses to mailshots can vary dramatically. I have worked on mailing campaigns where 1% of the list has responded to a message or offer and on other campaigns where

60% of the list has responded. What I can guarantee though is that if you embark on mailing thousands of people with no prior testing, you can end up with a zero response. I have seen this happen with many mailshots.

Measuring the Impact

It can be rather difficult to measure the impact upon your business of an individual mailshot in financial terms only. Of course, the ultimate aim of any direct mail campaign is to increase the number of sales and so comparing the value of the new business with the cost of the campaign is what determines its success or otherwise. However, as discussed earlier in the chapter, the reason behind some mailshots is to increase awareness of your business with cold prospects. Receiving new sales from these targets may be months or even years away and therefore the success of the mailshot is really determined by how many of the targeted recipients are moved to the next stage of the Continuum of Behaviour.

As a general guide, however, I have listed below some methods that can be used to measure the success of a mailshot from which increased sales is the primary objective.

o   Tracking the responses that you get from each mailshot.

o   Analysing how many of these responses actually convert to sales. (A response may be a positive indication of an intention to purchase, but it is not a sale.)

o   Making sure that you always identify where your responses are coming from so that you can see if one group is more responsive to an approach made by direct mail than another group.

    o   Keep a record of the costs of each campaign so you know how much this new business is costing you.

Good luck with any campaign that you embark upon.

5 MAKE YOUR ADVERTISING PAY

Whilst browsing in a gift shop I couldn't help but overhear the owner on the telephone, expressing her dismay that the £300 she had spent on a small advert in her local newspaper had not resulted in any responses. I asked her what she had hoped to achieve from this advertising. Sales were sluggish and she was hoping that advertising would bring new customers through the door. When I looked at her advert, it was no more than a business card. All it did was promote the name of her business and her address. In a sea of other adverts, some good, some bad and some just plain boring, her advert was lost and it was no wonder that new customers had failed to materialise.

Many small businesses use this hit and miss approach to advertising because they don't know any better. Why should they? It has taken me over 20 years to understand how to harness the full power of advertising. Along the way I have attended numerous seminars and workshops, read scores of books and of course made my own share of mistakes.

So, in this chapter we're going to tackle what to do to ensure that your advertising pulls in the required responses. This means covering the following:

- The benefits of advertising for a small business
- The key reasons why some small business adverts don't work
- Why an advertising plan is essential
- The golden rules for researching and negotiating
- Step-by-step copywriting

- DIY design, or bring in the experts?
- Measure, measure, measure!

The Benefits of Advertising for a Small Business

- **Increased sales.** With the right advertising, you can recover your costs and gain new clients for your business. In some cases, you'll go on to form long-term relationships with these clients so that the cost of acquiring them through advertising will seem quite low by comparison.

- **People that have responded to your advert** are expressing an interest in doing business with you. This pipeline of warm leads is of far greater value than a list of cold contacts simply because they are contacting you rather than the other way round.

- **Wide reach** - as a small business, you can't get in front of every potential client to sell your wares. The right publication however can put you in front of hundreds or thousands of potential new clients.

The Key Reasons Why Some Small Business Adverts Don't Work

As a small business, it is unlikely that you will have money to burn so spending money on advertising simply to create a positive impression of your business is a luxury you can ill afford.

You need to recover any advertising expense at the very least with the resulting new sales, and of course you should really be aiming for a profit.

I have worked in large organisations where vast sums of money were spent on advertising with the sole aim of "creating an intention to purchase." This is all well and good when you have a big budget that's spread across many different marketing activities, but as a small business with a more limited budget every pound that you spend has to deliver a return.

Here are the main reasons why so many small-business adverts fail:

- **The selected publication is not the right choice.** Maybe there are insufficient readers to pull in the responses or the readers are simply not interested in your products or services. You could be up against a competitor that advertises in the publication on a regular basis with a more attractive advert and a stronger message. The publication itself may not be up to scratch. If there is a distinct lack of interesting, topical and lively content, then no matter how good your advert is, it will not receive the necessary attention from readers.

- **The publication may be a great choice** but the cost of advertising is so high that achieving a cost-effective return is virtually impossible.

- **The advert itself is unimaginative** and doesn't enthuse the reader. Even worse, it looks amateurish with spelling mistakes and clumsy sentences. The attention it does attract is likely to be negative.

- **The advert looks great and reads well,** but it lacks a clear call to action. The reader, and your potential next client, turns over the page because they don't know what to do next.

- **Size!** So little space available that the advert results in being no more than a business card or, conversely, information overload - so much text that the reader isn't sure where to start and so moves on without bothering to find out.

Why an Advertising Plan Is Essential

Achieving advertising success lies in practical planning, good negotiation skills and bags of focused creativity!

It's a good idea with any marketing activity to spend some of your time on planning if you want to get results on a small budget. As a general rule of thumb, it should take you no more than four hours to scope out a simple but powerful advertising plan. I guarantee that if you spend time on putting together an advertising plan, you will save time and money further down the line.

How? Well, imagine the scenario: the telephone rings and on the other end is an advertising sales person offering you an unbeatable one off price for a space in their publication. Instead of being tempted to reach for your chequebook immediately, you will stop, pause and ask…

"Will advertising in this publication enable me to achieve the objectives I have defined in my advertising plan?"

If the answer is no, you will politely decline the offer.

A lack of planning means you can spend money in a spontaneous manner. If your sales are sluggish it can be tempting to part with small, or even large, sums of money in the hope that the space you are buying will close your sales gap and deliver a miracle. If your sales are buoyant, it can be just as tempting to spend money on advertising simply because you are feeling euphoric and on the crest of a wave with a little surplus cash.

Neither approach is right for your business if you are to achieve marketing success on a shoestring budget.

So, what are the components of your advertising plan?

I have listed here a number of points to consider. Make sure that you personalise each one for your business and write down any further thoughts that you may have. Spend some time thinking about your answers carefully.

- **Sales objectives.** This is the big one! What kind of measurable return (sales) are you looking to achieve from your advertising efforts? It can be tempting to write down figures that look inspiring, but are they realistic? Once you have got the costs of advertising in front of you, start to look at how much business you will need to cover these costs and how much business will provide you with a profit. These figures are your sales objectives. You may be happy with simply breaking even if you have a business where clients buy from you over a period of time. A new client would therefore herald the beginning of a long-term profitable relationship. On the other hand, you may want to make a clear profit because you have a business where clients buy once and once only. The great thing about establishing sales objectives is that when you start to look at advertising, you are either going to discount publications because it's impossible to break even let alone make a profit, or know that advertising in that specific publication is appropriate because the costs are reasonable and you are confident about reaching your sales objectives.

- **Target audiences.** You don't want to communicate to just any old reader; you want your advert to communicate to readers that could become potential clients. Having a genuine need for your products and services is vital if you are to be successful. It's really helpful at this stage to go back to your marketing plan (Chapter 1), in which you identified your target audiences. Make a list of the businesses and organisations that you want to reach and the people behind each one. You need to build up a picture of the individuals that you want to engage with. What do they do? What do they already know and believe about your products or services? How can you describe them? By their job title, hobby, their position of influence, membership of a professional body and so on? Having a clear and thorough understanding of the individuals you would like to reach in each organisation is going to help you when you start to look at the many publications in the marketplace. Rather than simply opting for a publication because it looks attractive and is offering a tempting deal, you will focus instead on whether this publication will lead you to your target readers in sufficient quantities to generate the responses that you need.

- **Content.** What do you want to say and promote in your advert? What will your compelling messages be? At this stage of your planning, you're not writing your advert, you're simply establishing the foundations. Get this right and the copy that follows will be focused, targeted and absolutely spot on!

Some questions to ask yourself when considering the content of your advert are:

Do you want to

o   Promote the launch of your new products/services?

o   Communicate the fact that you have a genuinely innovative product or service?

o   Showcase your products and services as being the best in their marketplace?

o   Let readers know that you have a genuine offer that you are making available to a limited number of new clients?

o   Promote the fact that you have a fantastic new website that you know will play a key part in converting warm leads into clients?

o   Tell readers that you have recently won some prestigious awards as a result of your customer service ethos and great products?

o   Communicate that business has grown substantially in recent months and introduce the new members of your team?

Allow yourself some quality thinking time and you will arrive at the foundations for a great advert.

- **Timing.** Generally speaking, the businesses that I work with do not make a random decision to advertise. They consider what is happening in their business in the next 12 months that could be given some extra punch by a well-timed advertising campaign. Some only advertise when they have a new product to launch or are improving their services. Others advertise when they have genuine special offers and want to bring in new clients by highlighting these. Maybe you have some old stock taking up space that will soon be required by new lines. A timely advert may help to shift it more quickly. There are many reasons why an advert at the right time can be more effective than an advert bought simply because you were caught at a weak moment by the advertising sales executive.

- **Budget**. There are many schools of thought on the subject of how much you should spend on advertising and whether you should set a budget beforehand. You can if you wish set an advertising budget for your business and base it as a small percentage of your existing turnover (usually this ranges from 1% to 10%) If you are a new business you will need to base this on your projected turnover. However, I wouldn't advise that you establish a budget for advertising on this basis until you are extremely confident that advertising rather than other marketing activities is going to be the route that will generate the most sales for your business.

The small businesses that I work with do their homework on the publications they are considering advertising in, they calculate the costs of advertising in each publication, and they draw up a shortlist of two to four publications that fit their criteria. Their final decision is based on the fact that they are confident of achieving their sales objectives. It then comes down to taking a prudent view of whether to run with the full shortlist or prune it further and test the waters. After going through this process, they arrive at an initial budget based on the total costs involved with advertising in the selected publications. This is a sensible approach. You can always increase your advertising budget when you know it works.

- **Design.** It's time to be honest about your design capabilities now. It's usually a good idea to ask a graphic designer to create your advert (something that we cover in more detail later) and if you're going to use images, ask a professional photographer to work wonders with your subject matter. Your own homemade design and digital images could result in seriously underselling yourself. Also, if you know what you want to say but you're not sure how to say it, then engaging a copywriter is sensible.

At this stage you're not actually parting with money. By spending time creating an advertising plan, you are ensuring that any advertising that you do embark upon will be targeted, timely and cost-effective. This strongly increases the likelihood of it being successful.

The Golden Rules for Researching and Negotiating

So, you've got your advertising plan scoped out. It's time now to start putting it into action by researching some appropriate publications. You will then start chatting to the advertising sales people responsible for each title and they will send you copies of their publications. Rate each publication against the work you did in your advertising plan before negotiating some great deals. You will finally arrive at the one or two publications that you're going to advertise in. But first things first... research.

Identify the titles that may be appropriate for you to advertise in.

o Ask your existing clients what titles they read. If they read more than one publication, which ones do they prefer? This will give you a feel for the publications that are likely to be read by other businesses in the same sectors as your clients.

o Use the Internet to search for publishing houses and individual publications with titles that you think could reach potential new clients. I have advertised in many publications found simply through spending an hour or so on Google.

o When you are chatting to cold prospects, ask them what publications they read. This is also a good way to engage in conversation when cold calling or networking.

o Find out from your local Chamber of Commerce, Business Link, or your local library if they can point you in the direction of media lists.

o Take a look at the Audit Bureau of Circulations website (*www.abc.org.uk*). This website includes a useful list of good publishing houses, together with the publications under the same umbrella.

Talking to the advertising sales executives

You've done your research and got your list of publications. Time now to pick up the phone and do some fact-finding on each one. Make sure that, above all else, you request copies of each publication.

• **Ask the advertising sales executive** responsible for each title to explain in detail the profile of readers that receive the publication. You need to refer back to your advertising plan in which you defined your target audiences. A good publishing house will be able to share a detailed breakdown of their readership profile.

- **Is the publication ABC (Audit Bureau of Circulations) audited?** When you actually get a copy of the publication in your hands, you will be able to tell this from the contents page. The letters ABC and a figure detailing the average net distribution of the publication will be present.

- **How is the publication distributed** and over what geographic area? Does it land on the desks of named decision-makers? Is it posted to a home address or a business address? Does the Royal Mail deliver the publication within defined postcode areas? Is it handed out at business networking groups or left in areas that attract heavy footfall where people can pick up a copy? It is really important that you understand from the advertising sales executive how the publication is distributed. There is a big difference between one publication that is left in batches for people to grab and another that reaches the reader by a more personal method of delivery.

- **Do they publish any other titles?** In many cases they will be responsible for a large number of publications and not just the title that is on your list. For example Haymarket Publications have numerous business and marketing titles under their banner while Hamerville Magazines Ltd has a range of titles that reach plumbers, electricians, builders, motor mechanics, motor factors and builders merchants.

- **Ask for the rate card of each publication.** This is a document that lists the price of each advert based on its size and position within a publication, and whether one space is bought or more. It is a good idea to measure the actual space so you know how much, or indeed how little, you could be getting for your money.

- **Is the publication paid for or is it free?** Don't be put off from advertising if the publication is free of charge. In my experience free publications can deliver excellent responses providing that the distribution is effective and the content is engaging to readers. This is especially true of local magazines that deliver regularly to local readers.

- **Is there a website that supports the publication** with an online community of readers? A growing number of publications are now targeting both new and existing readers via their website, along with forums and blogs. Find out if your advert will benefit from these additional channels and if they make an extra charge for the privilege of advertising online.

- **For each publication make sure that you** enquire whether they have a forthcoming features schedule. You may want to coincide your advertising with a special feature that brings more attention to your advert.

Evaluate each publication

The postman has been wearily tramping up your garden path for several days bringing large envelopes stuffed with magazines, journals, newspapers and accompanying rate cards. It's tempting to simply flick through each one. But don't! Time to stand in the shoes of the reader and really evaluate the publication through their eyes (and of course through your own eyes as a potential advertiser).

- **What does the publication look like?** How appropriate is the look of it to the targeted readers? For example, a trade magazine aimed at motor mechanics does not need to look glossy and slick to deliver results, whereas a publication aimed at architects needs to be a high-quality publication, stylish with eye-catching images.

- **Content is king!** Just how interesting and varied is the content? A publication with interesting, up-to-date and lively content is going to be harder for a reader to put down than one that is full of adverts with the odd bit of editorial thrown in for good measure. If you want your advert to be widely read, then it is important that it's featured in a publication that encourages readers to read, rather than one that is skimmed through before landing in the bin. If readers are skimming the content, they'll bypass your advert.

- **How many of your competitors are already in the magazine?** It may not concern you that existing competitors are also advertising, but if their budget extends to large adverts and yours doesn't, you could be at a disadvantage.

It's time now to negotiate

So, you've done your homework and by now you've discounted the publications that don't satisfy the stringent requirements and objectives that you've laid down in your advertising plan. Now pick up the phone and negotiate with the publications that appear to be most suitable.

Most publications will offer you their standard rate card, but in many cases the rate card is open to negotiation and in my experience, it does pay to negotiate!

The publication may have reached its full advertising quota so you won't have any bargaining power, or they may have a standard policy of always charging at full rate card, which is rare but not unheard of. Usually however, advertising fees can be reduced if you are willing to negotiate.

So, how can you negotiate? Here are some suggestions:

- **You can offer to pay a figure close** to the rate card, but request a decent piece of free editorial to be thrown in. Ask whether the publication can include your own press release (See Chapter 7 for details on how to create press releases and news pieces) or check whether they will write a small feature about your business. When negotiating, it's important that you revisit your advertising plan in which you identified why you want to advertise. This should influence the content of the free piece. For example, if you've recently won an award or gained an accreditation, the feature should ideally focus on this. In doing so it will really add value to your advert.

  Ask how many words they are willing to allow. Don't settle for anything less than 200, plus a decent accompanying image relevant to you, your business, or your products and services. Anything less than 200 words, and your feature could be overlooked. If you do go ahead, make sure that your advert alerts readers to your additional feature. One of my clients placed a double-page advert in a plumbing magazine and asked for a free full-page feature in the same issue. The feature was to consist of the in-house expert plumber putting my client's product through its paces. The magazine agreed and over 200 readers responded to the testing article alone, in addition to 400 from the advert itself. Be cheeky where free editorial is concerned.

- **Buy one get one free!** In return for placing one advert, ask for a second one in the next issue free of charge. If there is a separate price for advertising online, ask if they will throw in some online advertising for free. Always make sure that you agree the amount of free online space beforehand, however, so that you don't end up with space the size of a postage stamp.

- **Find out the final deadline for submitting adverts.** Contact the publication a day or two before this date and make an offer of up to 50% below the rate card price. If you're feeling bold, go for a quarter of the rate card price. At this stage, if the publication has not reached its revenue targets, it will be happy to consider your offer. Most publications aim to sell 100% of their available income generating space before going to print. In advertising circles, this is sometimes referred to as "distress space". It can be a risky strategy if you're pinning your hopes on appearing in the publication.

  You also need to be ready with your advert. You don't want to negotiate a great deal and then fall down at the next hurdle by submitting a hastily assembled advert that doesn't do your business any justice. But once you've created a great advert, by all means try this approach. It's one that I have used with success on many occasions.

- **Simply make an offer that you can comfortably afford.** If this is your very first advert in the publication, the chances are they will want to build a long-term relationship with you. This means that you can often negotiate a good deal on your first, second or even third advert. Again though, if you don't ask, they won't offer.

One small-business owner that I work with was offered an advert in a national newspaper for £800. He came back to the advertising sales executive with the price that he could afford which was just £200. His offer was accepted and the advert paid for itself many times over. So don't be shy about giving this a try.

When negotiating, always ask for your advert to feature on the right-hand page and check that you are not appearing on the same page as a competitor. When you actually place the business, ask for this to be confirmed in writing. Adverts that are placed on a right-hand page usually attract more eye contact than adverts placed on a left-hand page.

At this stage by all means negotiate a great deal, but don't immediately sign up. Allow a little time to make the final decision as to which publication or publications you are going to advertise in.

Draw up your shortlist

So finally, draw up a shortlist of the publications that you believe will work for your business. These will be publications that match your strong business hunch, that have been thoroughly researched and from which you believe you will get a return that will both cover your costs and make you a profit. But before finally committing to any deal

o Refer back to your advertising plan and those crucial sales objectives. Go through the cost benefit analysis of advertising in each publication, as your costs are likely to vary from publication to publication. How many sales do you need to break even? How many sales do you need to make a profit? Using your experience and knowledge of your business you need to decide whether these figures are attainable or pie in the sky.

o Now look at those advertising costs closely. It's time to decide how much of your precious marketing budget you are going to test on advertising. I use the word test, because this is what it should be - testing the waters, evaluating the response and then deciding whether further action is desirable.

o As a general rule of thumb, I will recommend to a client that they initially try a maximum of three publications. However, one advert in one publication is as good a start as any!

o If you get a fantastic response from one advert in one publication, you can then look at placing a second advert within the same publication and so on. I am a firm believer that every advert has to pay its way. Dipping your toe in the water with one advert in a thoroughly researched publication is therefore sensible.

o It's much easier to build on your advertising successes step-by-step than it is to invest in several adverts all at once. You will have the opportunity to identify what does work and what does not. This will in turn help you to avoid wasting money on adverts that only ever have a poor chance of success.

One of my clients places a series of quarter page adverts in two key trade magazines. He buys four adverts over a 12- month period and because of this upfront commitment, he has managed to negotiate a fantastic deal, including plenty of free press releases and competitions to support his adverts. However, he initially tested the waters with just one advert. After evaluating the response to this first advert, only then did he commit to a second advert. The response increased with the second advert and at that point, with the offer on the table of generous free editorial he progressed to a series of four adverts a year. He has secured thousands of pounds worth of free editorial and this has more than recovered the cost of advertising. The combination of adverts and editorial has proved to be a winning one and a substantial profit has been generated.

Step-by-Step Copywriting

You can do your research to find the publications that will lead to your target audiences. You can negotiate some exceptional deals. But if you run with an advert that looks dreary and uninspiring, that doesn't communicate clearly all that is good about your business in a language that the reader understands, then you're not going to get the results that you hope for. So, let's look at how we can be really creative and put together an advert that demands to be read and encourages people to respond. Before we move onto writing great copy, let's consider two different formats that our advert could take.

1) **The traditional advert that tells the** reader about an organisation's products or services. In addition to showing images and sharing some benefits, it tells the reader how they can find out more. This is probably the most common type of advert found in newspapers, journals, trade publications and magazines today. It can range in size from a fraction of a page to a double page spread.

2) **The advert that doesn't look like an advert,** but like an article instead. Unlike the content of a genuine news article or press release, this advert will include a number of focused selling messages and, if it's really good, a clear

and simple call to action. The reader may or may not be aware that they are in fact reading an advert. This is an increasingly popular way of advertising using a "soft sell" approach where the reader enjoys reading the article and before they know it, they are picking up the phone or visiting the company's website to find out more. These types of advert are more likely to vary in size from half a page to a double-page spread.

We will consider the copywriting appropriate to these two differing styles of adverts in the following steps.

Your Six Steps to Copywriting Success

Each one of these six steps is focused on getting reader responses. Ultimately, whilst it is wonderful to attract praise and flattery for your advert, marketing on a shoestring is all about generating the high level of interest in your product or services that leads to sales.

Step one: ask for help from the publication in which you're advertising

Ask the advertising sales executive for the recommended minimum and maximum word counts for the space that you have bought. If you're planning to use pictures or graphics, let them know how many and their approximate size so that they can confirm how much space will be left for your words. The number of words will vary according to the type of advert you are placing. For example, if you have bought a space for an article you should aim to include between 450 and 550 words for an A4 sized space. This allows for up to three small visuals.

If you have bought space for a traditional advert that will include a mixture of visuals, words and your contact details, then filling it with too much text is likely to be a mistake. Your advertising contact should have bags of experience in this area. Ask to be shown examples of adverts for the same sized space that you are buying. You can then be guided by what has worked well in the past.

Step two: make a list of the key selling points that you need to communicate

You are passionate about your business and this needs to be communicated in your advert. So what are the key benefits that will make a potential customer stop and take notice of your advert? Refer back to your advertising plan in which you mapped out the reasons why you want to advertise under your 'content' heading. It's also a good idea to ask your existing clients what attracted them to your business. Why not ask your suppliers, friends, family and networking peers for feedback too. Make a list of their comments. Revisit the readership profile to make sure that your messages will be completely relevant and engaging. Then make a small list of the powerful benefits that you're going to include.

o Ensure that benefits are clearly communicated. For example,

"Effective Time Management Training for business owners *that will free up one hour every single day.*"

"Permanent coolant leak repair - *guaranteed to last for the lifetime of the engine*"

o If you have a genuine unique selling point, make sure that you include this but always be truthful. The Advertising

Standards Authority (*www.asa.org.uk*) does not look kindly on adverts that are misleading and neither will your competitors.

o   If you have won awards, gained recognised qualifications, landed a prestigious contract, have sole distribution rights to a product or service, then you should be looking to include these facts within your advert. They can help you to stand apart from your competitors and they encourage readers to find out more.

o   How does your service stand up to scrutiny? Is there anything about the way in which you service your clients that makes you stand apart from your competitors? If the answer is yes, you should be talking about your service in your advert.

o   Return to your advertising plan and the publications on your shortlist. What do the readers of each publication already know and believe about your products or services? Is there anything happening in your marketplace right now that if communicated to the readers will motivate them to act? When looking at the benefits to include in your advert, keep these readers firmly in mind.

At this point, try and keep to one or two sheets of bullet points so that you are not overwhelming yourself with too much information. You will then have a great reference point when it comes to writing the content of your advert.

Step three: decide on your clear call to action

I have seen a large number of great adverts fall down at this hurdle. Does the reader know how to find out more? Regardless of the size of your advert, you need a clear call to action. For example, do you want the reader to

o Visit your website to download some free useful information or some top tips? To read a White Paper or your latest newsletter? To enter a simple quiz, view your latest offers or see your latest catalogue?

o Pick up the phone and call you to arrange a meeting, or to request a survey, a free guide or your brochure?

o Visit your blog and add their comments?

o Attend your free seminar?

Whatever you want the reader to do, it's vital that your advert clearly communicates this. Just one word of warning, there is nothing to be gained from asking readers to do something unrealistic. For example, I was recently asked to appraise an advert that had failed to pull in a single response, even though it was beautifully laid out with all the right messages. The problem was that the call to action entailed the business owner asking readers to attend a high level one to one financial consultation. This was a step too far given that the relationship was a cold one. He would have been much better off asking readers to phone or e-mail for more information, or to visit his website to sign up for his newsletter and find out more. Make sure that your call to action is both clear and realistic.

Step four: consider increasing responses with an offer

This is an old advertising trick. The secret lies in ensuring that any offer is relevant to your business, that you can afford it and, most importantly, that the reader will see it as a genuine and appealing offer. Offering for example a cheap throwaway pen to encourage readers to phone you or visit your website may do you more harm than good. If you're not sure, there's nothing like asking your existing clients for their thoughts on any ideas.

You can go further with the offer and restrict it to the first 20 readers to respond, or go further still and have a closing date on the offer to encourage readers to act quickly. Procrastination can cost you good responses so a close date can be a good way of combating this. Any close date you impose needs to allow sufficient time for the publication to be distributed. I have come across adverts where the close date has passed even though the publication has only just been circulated.

To illustrate how offers can work here are examples of adverts that I have placed for small businesses:

"A free IT review worth £180 plus a bottle of Champagne for the first five businesses to take out an IT support contract."

"A 20% discount on your business stationery including letterheads, business cards and compliment slips if you place your order by 30th September."

"A free mug and drinks coaster for every single reader that returns their completed survey by the close date."

"Visit our website today to download your free copy of 'How to Get on the Front Page of Google.'"

"A complimentary one-to-one coaching session for the first 10 readers to contact us."

Step five: grab reader attention with a great headline

Many small business owners find the headline to be the hardest part of writing an advert. Rest assured, it's not that difficult and I will show you how to write a great headline. We are all capable of writing headlines, some good, some excellent and some brilliant. We all just need a little practice!

The headline really is the most important part of your advert. It has the difficult job of catching the reader's attention and then holding their interest long enough for them to take on board the messages that follow. You don't have to worry about creating a headline that is truly original. Most of the great headlines that you see are a combination of popular sayings or slogans, or they are existing headlines with a few tweaks. Never copy a headline, but you can be inspired by it if you believe it is relevant to the messages in your advert.

So, how do you get started? Here are some suggestions:

- **Start by jotting down headlines** that appeal to you when you're out and about or even sitting in front of the television. This means being equipped at all times with a pen and a pad! Becoming aware of what you like and don't like means that you are beginning to tune yourself in to a creative way of thinking. And creativity is at the heart of all great headlines.

- **Make a list of the powerful words** and phrases that you, and indeed your clients and suppliers, would associate with your business. What are the positive words that you use to describe your business to potential clients?

- **Time now to invest a few pounds** in a flip chart pad and some colourful pens. Map out your initial thoughts for headlines based on the work that you have done and the benefits you want to communicate. If the thought of doing this alone does not appeal, include some creative friends that can provide sparkle and inspiration in exchange for some decent hospitality. Share your ideas around the table. A nice big space where you can write freely, using lots of different colours is a great way to engage the creative side of your brain. So let's start looking at building that headline.

The words 'you' and 'your' are very important when writing headlines, far more important than 'me', 'us' or 'I'. So, if you can use these words then you will draw attention to the whole headline. Don't worry if you can't, just make sure that the rest of your text is sprinkled with them.

If you are making a genuine offer, then one technique is to use the headline to communicate that offer and if you can combine it with a number, even better. For example:

" Discover The 7 Secrets to Growing Your Business on the Web"

" Download Your Free Copy of 'How to Reduce Your Tax Bill in 3 Easy Steps' Now"

"4 Compelling Reasons Why You Should Buy Our Promotional Gifts"

You can create a headline with a question.

"Are You Looking for a New Accountant?"

"Would You like to Increase Your Online Sales by 100%?"

147

If your offer is unbeatable, your product fantastic or your range of products award-winning, then bring those words into your headline.

"Now You Can Buy Our Award-Winning Luxury Cakes Online"

"You Won't Ever See This Unbeatable Offer Again"

You can even create a headline with testimonial from one of your delighted clients but substantiate it in the text that follows:

"The Best Customer Service We Have Ever Had"

"No Other Stationery Company Has Ever Come Close on Service"

Hopefully this will help you to arrive at some headlines. If your ideas dry up for the day, don't worry. Simply sow the thought in your mind and you will be surprised by the ideas that will randomly crop up as you go about your everyday tasks. The fact is that you have started the creative process and good headlines will surely follow.

How long should your headline be?

This debate has raged in marketing and advertising circles for decades - is a short headline more effective than a long one or vice versa? Of course the amount of space available can impact the length of the headline, but ultimately it is the quality rather than the quantity that determines its success. Here are a few short advertising headlines that I have written for small businesses. See what you think!

o   Do You Want To Be Whiter Than White?
   (For a dental practice promoting teeth whitening)

o   When Things Go Bump in the Night
     (For a security business keen to promote their night-time service to other businesses)

o   Outsource Your Payroll and Then Relax
     (For a payroll bureau)

o   The Fab Four
     (For motor products specialists showcasing four of their products)

o   Not Just a Pretty Face… Why HH Design Go beyond Just Great Looks

o   Art for Art's Sake? …. Never! Why HH Design Fuse Purpose with Passion
     (For design agency, HH Design, marketing their focus on results driven design)

o   Beating the Space Invaders…
     (For local warehousing and archiving specialists advertising to businesses tight on space)

These headlines don't use complicated phrases and are catchy enough to grab attention. Great headlines should simply consist of ordinary everyday words that work well together and are attractive on the eye.

I will leave the final words on headlines to Richard Bowler, Group Editor at Hamerville Magazines Limited and a dab hand when it comes to writing headlines. He says, "Headline writing is an important part of putting together an advert. Many newspapers employ staff to write headlines so it shows their value. The headline is one of the first things to catch the eye of the reader so it's vital that you keep it snappy and if appropriate, use humour. A good headline will draw the reader in and make them curious about reading the text that follows. There are many influences that can inspire you when deciding on your headline such as well-known sayings or phrases or even film or song titles. Never spend too long over a headline. It's amazing how many times you get the headline you want when you are not forcing the issue."

So, let loose your creative spirit and enjoy constructing some cracking headlines.

Step six: make the content interesting, inspiring and relevant

You know the beginning of your advert, your headline and you know the end of your advert, which is your call to action. We are now going to focus on the bit in between! Try to think of your advert as a story. Most good stories have a beginning, middle and an end. They take the reader on a journey. This is what you want to do with your advert whether you are publishing a traditional advert or an advert in the article style. It is time now to refer to the sheet of benefits that you created earlier and to your advertising plan in which you outlined why you want to advertise. You need to be communicating benefits here - benefits that the readers, your target audience, will connect with and find relevant. Remember to keep talking to the reader as if they were in front of you. That means referring to you rather than to we.

- **Once you have ascertained** from your advertising sales executive the number of words you have to play with, your content should then focus on presenting a small number of powerful benefits, plus any particular achievements, accolades or awards. As discussed earlier, any genuine offers and close dates can also be included.

- **You can add some extra sparkle** with a few lines of testimonial from a very satisfied customer or two. It will help if your satisfied customer shares a similar profile to the readers and they go beyond simply saying that your services or products are wonderful. If you saved them money, the testimonial should refer to how much. If you've massively improved their business, the testimonial should describe just how. Facts, figures and statistics are really powerful when they are coming from a happy customer.

- **How many benefits to communicate?** It does depend on the number of words available to you but if you're squashing benefits in, then you need to use a red pen and take some out. Less is definitely more in a small advert and two or three powerful benefits will stand out, whereas six or seven could make your advert unreadable.

Tips for Writing an Article Style Advert

If you need some extra inspiration when it comes to writing an article style advert, then here are two effective, yet simple approaches:

- **Why not arrange to be interviewed?** Find someone appropriate to interview you, such as the head of your networking group, a high-profile person within your business community that you know on a personal level, or a great client that you have a long-standing relationship with. It is important that the content is interesting and genuine. Interviews are regularly read so they are a great way to get the attention of readers. Aim for six interesting questions and make sure your answers are just as interesting. If you try to oversell yourself, readers will be put off. They want to find out why you started your business, what you do, whether you do anything differently to your competitors and the types of clients that you work with. Don't go in to too much personal detail about your hobbies and what you like for breakfast! If you're stuck for questions, read the interviews in the business supplements of the high-quality Sunday newspapers and you will easily come up with half a dozen.

- **A top tips article**. The great thing about top tips articles is that they are much easier to write than the traditional narrative style articles that you often read in publications. You simply dispense useful information in a series of tips and conclude with a reader offer and your contact details. If you like the idea of writing a top tips article, have a good read of Chapter 7 where this subject is explored in detail.

When getting down to the nitty-gritty of actually writing your article style advert, sketch it out with your beginning, middle and end. Add your text and play around with words and phrases before you actually start typing. When your first draft is typed up, get out your red pen and read through it again, making any changes necessary to improve it further. Show the draft to a few friends or colleagues before arriving at a final draft that is good enough to frame!

Regardless of the style of your advert

Always do your final checks on a printed copy. It's much easier to check from a piece of paper than it is from your computer screen where you are likely to overlook small errors. Whatever you do, make sure that when you receive a proof of your advert from the publication, you check it thoroughly against the text that you sent. Small errors can creep in at proof stage so don't assume that what you receive is either word perfect or picture perfect. You will be expected to sign off the final proof as being accurate and therefore print ready. It's no good complaining when the publication comes out if there's an error in your advert when you signed it off. Check each proof you receive with a fine toothcomb.

DIY Design, or Bring in the Experts?

I'm sure you've seen many homemade adverts in your time. You know the ones - fuzzy images, clipart boxes and a patchwork of colours and styles that don't bear any resemblance to the brand. Unless you are a designer yourself, it is advisable to employ one to create your adverts. It won't break the bank but it could make the difference between your advert getting responses or being ignored because it looks unprofessional. The shoestring philosophy can still be used here.

- **Ask the publication if they provide a design service.** Many will typeset your advert for a modest charge or even for free. If you are presenting your advert in an article style format, the charge for typesetting will usually be included in the cost of the space. But again, if you don't ask this is unlikely to be offered. Ensure that any images that you supply to the magazine, including your logo and business name, are of a high quality resolution and so don't look blurred when they are reproduced.

- **You may already be working with a designer** in which case ask for a fixed price quotation. If you don't have anyone in mind, ask around for a good designer and you will undoubtedly get many recommendations. Make your decision based on the quality of their previous work and the enthusiasm that they display when discussing your advert.

Measure, Measure, Measure!

Your advert has finally made it into the publication and it's now just a matter of waiting for those responses to come in. In order to understand the impact of your advert, you need to be able to identify those people that have contacted you as a result of it. Make sure that you ask every prospect that contacts you where they heard about you. I've worked with enough small businesses to know that tracking responses from advertising is not high on their agenda. Once the advert is published, they forget to think about this important aspect or only make a half-hearted effort. Do not make the same mistake.

- Keep a record of all responses triggered by each advert.

- Keep a record of the responses from each advert that actually converts to business. Responses are great, but it's hard business that counts and that ultimately determines how successful your advert has been.

- Keep a record of the lifetime value of each new client that comes from each advert. Compare the lifetime value of each client that you gain from advertising, with that of clients gained through other marketing channels.

- Has that lovely free PR you negotiated made a difference? Ask your new clients if they spotted your article as well as your advert.

It was Lord Leverhulme who famously said that half of his advertising budget was wasted, but he didn't know which half! Make sure that you understand exactly where your advertising budget has gone and what it has delivered. This way you won't be in danger of wasting any money.

6 EXHIBITION SKILLS TO BRING HOME THE BUSINESS

The chances are that the opportunity to market your business through an exhibition will be floated under your nose at some point. You may already have dipped your toes in the water and have a tale to tell.

The fact is that exhibitions can be fantastic for promoting your business to cold prospects, hot prospects and even existing clients. At the other end of the scale however, they can be a huge drain on your time and money and you can walk away with very little to show for your efforts. The secret lies in finding the right exhibition to showcase your wares and then pulling out all the stops where your marketing is concerned. And that means rolling up your sleeves and getting stuck into action long before the exhibition begins and long after it has ended.

When it comes to exhibitions, just a little marketing know how can help you achieve some great results.

In this chapter we are going to look at how you can use exhibitions as a powerful marketing tool and that means covering the following:

- The common exhibition mistakes made by small businesses
- How to identify the right exhibition for your business
- Small can be beautiful
- Planning for success
- Developing a simple but powerful action plan
- Your exhibition marketing tool kit
- Running your exhibition stand on the day

- Essential influencing skills that really work
- The importance of doing your sums afterwards

The Common Exhibition Mistakes Made by Small Businesses

Before considering how to get the most from exhibitions, let's start by covering some of the common mistakes that can lead to an exhibition being a waste of time and money rather than a generator of new business.

- **Failure to research the exhibition itself** to determine whether it is the right forum and venue to attract the correct profile of hot and cold prospects. Don't be swayed by the sales patter from the organisers, look at the hard business facts.

- **Pitching up on the day** of the exhibition with crossed fingers hoping that sufficient people will come through the doors.

- **Failing to view** the whole exhibition marketing process as a business development exercise, one that requires careful planning from start to finish.

- **Presenting a drab and unprofessional** exhibition stand. Rather than attracting visitors to it like a magnet, it will turn people off or be seen as just another of the bland and uninteresting stands already present.

- **Displaying defensive or unwelcoming body language** on the stand. Standing with arms folded, hovering to pounce or oblivious to any visitors while drinking from a bottle, is not how you want to appear. Then there's the lure of that mobile phone and the endless cups of coffee that don't make for pleasant breath. It is an error to forget why you are at the exhibition and to let visitors become an unwelcome intrusion!

- **The exhibitor displays a tendency to be more interested** in talking about themselves to visitors rather than listening to what is being said. It's a matter of talk, tell and sell at the expense of building a healthy dialogue.

- **Packing up half an hour** before the end of the exhibition and missing out on the visitors that are running late. There are always some visitors that are genuinely looking for new suppliers and partners but have left things to the last minute.

- **Failing to capture sufficient or accurate details** from genuinely interested visitors through lack of concentration.

- **All of those lovely exhibition leads** that took so long to get on the day are simply not followed up! They sit in boxes gathering dust and several months down the line, they are still sitting in boxes until they eventually make their way to the recycling bin.

- **Booking new exhibitions without measuring** whether the previous one was a success. The perception of success should not be based on the number of visitors that attended the stand but on the actual business that was written afterwards.

Don't fall into these traps. With a positive mindset and a clear plan of action, you can steer clear of making these mistakes.

How to Identify the Right Exhibition for Your Business

As a small business, you need to consider carefully whether it is wise to sink any of your precious marketing budget into an exhibition. Therefore, before you get dazzled into signing up to an exhibition that has caught your eye, ask the following questions:

- **What is the theme of the exhibition** and how attractive does it look and sound to potential visitors? For example, is there a seminar programme? Is there a networking area that will encourage visitors and exhibitors alike to get together? How about Internet facilities for visitors and exhibitors, good-quality refreshments and a few good keynote speakers that will pull in the crowds? Is the venue attractive and spacious with good lighting? How easy is it to get to the venue? Is parking nearby for exhibitors and good transport links for visitors? Make sure that you consider these points when judging an exhibition. If the exhibition doesn't appeal to you then it is unlikely to appeal to visitors.

- **How much will it cost you to exhibit?** Don't simply look at the cost of the floor space that you will be buying. This is usually just the first charge in a long line of expenses. You may need to take the following into consideration:

  o Lighting and power for the stand
  o Rental of stand furniture and literature displays
  o Insurance
  o Additional staffing costs
  o Overnight hotel stays, meals, travel expenses and parking
  o Pop-up banners and other marketing collateral

When you start to list all the expenses, you may be surprised at the final figure that greets you. It's better to know what your final bill will be before you sign up to anything rather than receiving an unpleasant surprise after the event.

- **How are the organisers marketing the exhibition** to potential visitors? You will want to see visitors pouring through the doors and heading for your stand. So press the organisers on this question until you get hard facts and statistics in writing.

- **What is the profile of the visitors that are being targeted?** You need to ensure that the people coming through the door are likely to be potential clients that will be looking for your kind of products or services, or key influencers that can connect you to new clients. Again, the organisers should be able to tell you in detail who they are targeting and how.

- **Will any of your competitors be exhibiting?** It might not trouble you if you are in a room full of your competitors. But on the other hand you may not relish the idea. Either way, it's best to find out before you sign on the dotted line.

- **Can you look after your exhibition stand** on your own or will you need some help? Being stuck on your own for what can sometimes be a few long days isn't a joke and you soon start to lose your sparkle. Another pair of hands can make a huge difference.

- **Is the exhibition taking place at the weekend** or during the working week? You need to balance spending time away from your business with the potential benefits that you will gain from exhibiting.

Small Can Be Beautiful

If you're not sure where to start looking for opportunities to exhibit, why not begin your search close to home? By way of example, in Horsham, West Sussex, the Business Development Unit at the District Council organises an annual event called Horsham Microbiz™. This is an exhibition that is aimed at small businesses and people thinking of starting a business in the District. The cost of exhibiting is subsidised in part by the Council and by local business sponsors, so exhibitors have a very good opportunity to promote their products and services on a shoestring budget. Find out if your District Council organises local exhibitions like this one and if you draw a blank, why not ask if they will consider the idea? Whilst you're at it, get in touch with your local Chamber of Commerce and Business Link. These organisations should know what is happening locally and what exhibitions are planned throughout the year.

How about getting your networking group galvanised into action? The networking group I belong to organises an annual exhibition for which the cost of exhibiting is always kept within the scope of most small business budgets. In my experience and that of the many small businesses I come into contact with, local exhibitions can be very effective in generating warm leads and sales. They attract a local audience and when organised properly, have most of the benefits of the bigger national exhibitions including networking areas, decent refreshments and great speakers.

Time to make it all add up

Once you have the answers to these questions, you will arrive at the stage where you have calculated the vast majority of the costs of exhibiting, and will have a very good feel for the benefits.

It's then simply a matter of calculating how much business you need to generate from the exhibition to cover your costs and subsequently, how much business you need to generate to make a healthy profit.

Take a long hard look at the figures. What is the likelihood of you actually hitting those targets? Only you know the answer. You need to trust your business acumen and your gut feeling. If you arrive at the conclusion that you're not going to cover your costs or make a profit, then you should hold onto your marketing budget and save it for other activities that offer a much higher potential of yielding a profitable return. Saying 'no' can be as powerful as saying 'yes' and in the last 24 years I have turned down far more exhibitions than I have accepted.

Alternatively of course, if the figures look realistic then it's all stations go and on to the next stage of getting to grips with your exhibition stand.

Planning for Success

By now you will be familiar with the mantra of this book. It's all about planning and preparation. This is definitely the hallmark of marketing on a shoestring. Your biggest expense should always be your time. When it comes to exhibition planning, there are two important things to consider.

- **The Exhibition Checklist.** This is a document that I include in all of my Exhibition Skills workshops and one that I use without exception for every exhibition that I'm involved with. I've included a copy of it at the end of this chapter so that you can use it as the basis for your own exhibition to-do list. Simply copy what's useful, discard the rest and add in the additional details that are relevant to you. By using this little form and updating it regularly, you will avoid running around on the day of the exhibition itself asking your fellow exhibitors if they can lend you sticky tape, or cursing yourself for forgetting your prospect forms and diary.

- **The need for a knockout stand.** You don't need a huge stand to create a stunning display. I have worked with many small businesses whose stand comprised only of a rectangular table and some space at the back for a pop-up banner. Even with these limitations, they created a great looking stand that attracted visitors in their droves. The secret lies in being as creative as possible and not resorting simply to fanning out your literature and business cards and adding some sweets for people to grab as they go by.

You can create an attractive and welcoming stand from a table and some backspace quite easily. Here are some ideas:

- **Buy a couple of pieces of good quality** fabric in your corporate colours. Opt for plain colours with one of the pieces being large enough to reach the floor and cover your table completely. You can then use the space underneath your table for storage. The other piece of fabric should be twice the size that you need to cover the tabletop itself … read on!

- **Hunt out old shoeboxes and smaller sturdy boxes** in varying sizes. You are going to use these underneath your top cloth so that you add height and interest to your stand. You can then use these raised displays to showcase your literature and other items that will give your stand the wow appeal. If you fall into the trap of simply laying out literature and other items on a flat surface, you won't catch the eye of visitors as they are approaching. In fact a boring and flat display actually encourages people to walk by without a backward glance.

- **Think about what you display on your stand**. Anything that will add some interest, intrigue or anticipation will help you to strike up a conversation with visitors. For example, one client, a car valet company, used a new bucket with chamois leather for his business card draw. Another, an HR consultant, placed an attractive roll of red ribbon in the middle of her stand with a pair of scissors accompanied by the strap line 'With Our HR Services, We Cut through the Red Tape.' A telephone marketing company had four different telephones on their stand with a torn up script to communicate their non-scripted approach to telemarketing. Consider what tools and props you can use to show what you do and that could help you strike up a conversation.

- **A business card draw is a great way to get hold** of useful contact information. Make sure that you display the prizes on your stand if you're offering something really attractive such as champagne, lovely chocolates or other tempting goodies. If, however, the prize is a free trial of your services, then make an attractive list of the benefits that the winner will receive and laminate it so that visitors are encouraged to pick it up and read.

- **Get hold of some plastic business card** holders so that your business cards are not scattered in a mess about your stand. They only cost a few pounds and it's well worth investing in two or three and having them dotted around your stand.

- **Don't fall into the trap of placing bundles** of free promotional gifts on your stand that people can simply grab as they walk by. A little further into the chapter, we look at how you can make your promotional gifts pay for themselves many times over!

- **Once you have planned out exactly what** you are going to place on your table, you need to carry out a practice run with a space that matches the exact dimensions of your table. Don't wait until the day of the exhibition itself. Practice really does make perfect and the chances are that once you start dressing your table, you will be inspired with even more ideas. Then, when you eventually arrive at a layout that you're really happy with, sketch it out on a piece of paper and take it with you to the exhibition. This will help you no end when you are setting up.

- **If space is available at the back of your stand** for a display, then a pop-up banner is an inexpensive way of marketing your business. It creates another level of interest that will again help to attract visitors. Don't cram your banner with so much text that no one can read it. Focus instead on including three to six benefit driven bullet points about your business. Allow room for a couple of lines of client testimonial. What about some great images? Remember to include your website and contact details and make sure that the design is consistent with the look of your business and your corporate colours. Don't opt for a bargain basement pop-up banner. Buying one of these is like buying a cheap umbrella that you put to the test on a windy day. A good one, however, will last for several years.

- **Finally, when you have got everything together**, stand in the shoes of the people that will be visiting your stand and try to look at it through their eyes. Get a second opinion and then tick the boxes on your exhibition checklist. You've done a good job and it's now time to put together an action plan to ensure that your stand is the one most sought-after on the day.

Developing a Simple but Powerful Action Plan

Earlier on, we highlighted that one of the mistakes that a small business can make when exhibiting is to rely upon the organisers to generate sufficient visitor traffic to make exhibiting worthwhile. If you really want to make money from exhibiting, then you have to drum up your own visitors as well. By all means make every effort to grab the attention of the visitors that do turn up as a result of the organiser's efforts, but by generating your own traffic as well, you will guarantee a strong level of interest. How do you do this? Here are some suggestions:

- **Invite hot prospects, cold prospects** and clients to your stand. Make a wish list of the people that you would like to visit your stand. For example:

  o People that have expressed an interest in your services or products but they are yet to buy from you.

  o People that you've met on your business networking travels, and who could be useful contacts or even potential clients.

o People you've heard about on the business grapevine and have earmarked as good prospects for your business.

o Existing clients - it's always a good idea to keep in touch with your existing clients beyond a telephone call, an invoice or the occasional one-to-one meeting.

o Lapsed clients. This would be a good reason to get back in touch with them.

o Journalists or other media contacts. It's always a good idea to make connections with your local media if you are exhibiting at a local exhibition.

Who else can you invite? Spend an hour or so on your list and keep coming back to it. The last name that you write down could turn out to be your best client yet.

- **Make your invitations personal and memorable.** Sometimes the exhibition organisers will have pre-printed invitations that are really useful for communicating what is happening at the exhibition. I would recommend, though that you also add your own personal touch if you want to receive positive responses by the bucket load. It is well worth considering:

  o Creating a personal e-mail with an equally personal heading rather than an e-mail sent to everybody.

  o Getting on the phone to secure that precious diary space. This also provides the opportunity to maintain personal contact with a valued or lapsed client. Make sure that you follow up with a hand signed letter of invitation or a nice e-mail.

    o   Sending out a reminder a few days before the exhibition. If you are enthusiastic about the exhibition and how your guests will benefit from attending, then you're more likely to have a packed stand on the day itself.

- **Use promotional gifts as a hook**. Attend any exhibition and it is likely that that you will come across stands that are littered with promotional giveaways, from pens, mugs, clocks and key rings to USB sticks and coasters. This is great for visitors that are on a treasure trail, but as a small business, can you afford to give away gifts without making them actually pay for themselves? Rather than scattering them about like confetti, you can use promotional gifts in a creative and targeted way to pull in your target visitors.

For example, one small business client was exhibiting at a national exhibition that was traditionally well attended by many of the key business people that she wanted to do business with. She identified several business people that she really wanted to visit her stand. Accompanying the personal invitation she sent out was an attractive drinks coaster that was branded with her company details. The coaster was part of a five-piece desk set. The recipient was asked to bring the coaster along to the exhibition stand, where they would be given the remaining four pieces of the desk set. The result? Every person that was invited actually turned up and many prospects were converted into customers. This is a simple but effective approach.

At exhibitions aimed at trades people the offer of a free thermal drinks mug complete with teabags and biscuits always goes down well, as does the offer of a china mug filled with jelly beans or chocolates. If you really want those people on your guest list to come to your stand then use promotional gifts to encourage them. Don't be tempted to hand them out to anyone. Give free gifts to your hot prospects and targeted clients rather than people with empty carrier bags on the lookout for a freebie! You will find other ideas on how you can use promotional gifts in Chapter 4.

- **Let the media know you are exhibiting.** It always pays to ask the exhibition organisers if they have a press office where you can introduce yourself to their media contacts before sending them your press releases. Will there be a Press Room at the exhibition where you can leave press releases and company information for journalists to pick up? Often, exhibition organisers are on the hunt for interesting exhibitor stories that can be used to promote the event. Include media contacts on your invitation list and invite each journalist to visit your stand on the day itself. In Chapter 7, we cover the whole area of PR in detail.

- **When talking to the exhibition organisers why not** enquire if there are any opportunities for speaking? Many of the speakers at an exhibition are in fact exhibitors themselves. I always ask for a speaking slot when I am exhibiting, as it's a great way of bringing new people to your stand. If you are given a speaking opportunity, focus on sharing good advice and tips rather than simply plugging your business. Make sure that the audience knows where your stand is located so that they can visit you afterwards. Don't be surprised when a large number of people descend upon you, keen to find out more about what you do. You have wowed them with your words and it's your time to be rewarded.

- **Capturing individual visitor details on the day**. This is very important and here are some suggestions how to do this:

  o Bring along plenty of prospect forms - I have included a template at the end of this chapter. Make sure that you gather as much relevant information as possible about your prospect, including their specific need for your services and when they are likely to use you. Find out if they are the decision maker, or part of the decision-making team. If they are neither, ask for the details of the person that you should be speaking to and ask permission to use their name to help successfully navigate past the gatekeeper.

  o When you are gathering an individual's details, ask for permission to follow-up after the exhibition with an e-mail or a telephone call. Make a note on the prospect form that you have been given this consent. When you do follow-up you will not be making a cold call or sending an unwelcome e-mail.

  o Use your diary to book meetings on the day with interested prospects. Strike while the iron is hot! Many people are happy to arrange a meeting with you but if you don't suggest one, it won't happen. You can always make a provisional date if your prospect doesn't have their diary to hand on the day. People tend to be relaxed when they are at an exhibition and therefore more open to the prospect of a meeting.

- **Take time to follow-up your hot prospects** after the exhibition. It's no good having dozens of warm leads to follow-up if you haven't allocated the time in your diary to convert them into sales. Make sure that when you book the exhibition in your diary, you also allocate follow-up time after the exhibition to begin the process of turning warm leads into actual sales. Don't forget - this is what it's all about! Many small businesses don't do this and as a result they struggle to convert leads into business, and over time their enthusiasm for exhibiting wanes.

Four steps for a successful follow-up

If you have invested some of your marketing budget into an exhibition, it's vital that you get the most from it. This means following up with passion and persistence, so follow this simple process within a few days of the exhibition ending.

o Get on the telephone and confirm the meetings that you have booked, or book in meetings with the people who expressed interest.

o Send out any information that you promised.

o If you're not responsible for following up, then pass the leads through to the person who is. Don't just plonk them on their desk; give a thorough briefing on each prospect. This is the opportunity to justify your spend by securing new business.

o Follow up with everyone within three to five working days of the exhibition ending. You want people to remember their conversation with you. Don't wait for warm leads to go cold.

By adopting a thorough and proactive follow-up process you are well on the road to increasing your sales and getting a return on your spend.

Your Exhibition Marketing Tool Kit

By using marketing literature to promote your business at an exhibition you can achieve some remarkable results. And we're not talking glossy brochures that cost the earth. Decent quality letterhead paper is all that you really need. Here are some ideas of what to do with it:

- **A press release.** This is a great way to communicate interesting news about your business. I always encourage businesses to create a press release specifically for their exhibition stand. A press release is a simple way of presenting information in an attractive format that will grab attention. Chapter 7 covers how to write a press release in more detail.

- **Frequently asked questions and answers.** Stand in the shoes of your visitor and think about the questions they would probably like to ask about your business. Make sure that your answers are both helpful and inspiring. You won't necessarily get enough time on the day itself to speak at length with each person that visits your stand, so a question and answers handout can be a useful alternative. Produce it on your letterhead paper with no more than four or five questions per side of A4. If necessary, run to a couple of pages so that each question and answer has sufficient spacing to make it easy to read.

- **Client case studies.** Once you have your client's permission to write one, focus on telling an interesting story rather than selling. What did your client want? What did you deliver? How did you deliver it and finally, how did your client benefit from your services or products? A few lines of positive testimonial will add the finishing touch to each case study. Again, use your letterhead paper and stick to one case study only. This will have more impact than several case studies crammed on top of each other. If you visit my website, (*www.themarketinggym.org*) you will be able to use case studies that I have written as a guide.

- **A credentials document.** This is usually no more than two pages long in which you communicate the following information in clear and concise paragraphs:

  o The name of your business

  o The types of clients with whom you work

  o Your areas of expertise

  o Any relevant projects that you want to highlight

  o Your products and services

  o Any professional insurances and qualifications that you hold

  o Your contact details, including your website

  This is a useful document that will be welcomed by a potential client who is new to your business.

- **Create literature and promotional packs beforehand.** Gather everything together that you would like to provide to a prospective client, attach your business card, and pop it into an envelope with your company details on the front, including the name and date of the exhibition. Most of the literature given out at an exhibition ends up in a jumble in the free carrier bag provided. If your literature is in a sealed envelope, it increases the chances that it will be kept and read.

Running Your Exhibition Stand on the Day

It's not simply a matter of pitching up and putting up. There are a few tricks of the trade to follow when it comes to running your exhibition stand on the day and these tips will help you in your quest for new business.

- **Aim to get there as soon as you're allowed.** If you can set up your stand the day before, then it's a good idea to do this. You don't want to become flustered while setting up your stand on the morning. Things can go wrong and it's better to be able to rectify any problems the night before.

- **Be ready to greet people as they approach your stand** in the first few minutes of the exhibition opening. Fumbling around trying to locate your materials or your contact sheets can lose you that important potential client, whereas being ready and smiling could lead you to your next big sale.

- **Make sure that you talk to your fellow exhibitors** during the day. Being friendly and gregarious can lead to a new client from the most unexpected quarters.

- **Don't try to go it alone for the whole day** if you can avoid it. It's good to have someone with whom to share the highs and the lows, as well as help keep your stand fully attended all day long. There will also be busy periods, for example when the seminars empty out and your stand can suddenly become busy.

- **Smiling at people as they go by will help** you to appear friendly and approachable. Be careful to avoid overdoing this though as inane grinning can be rather disconcerting!

- **Don't eat or drink on your stand** and keep your phone out of sight. If you have to make calls, be disciplined and leave your stand. Do the same when you need refreshments.

- **Take a freshen-up-kit with you.** You will need it during the day because standing in a warm and busy environment can make you look stale, smell stale and feel stale.

- **Tidy up your stand as the day goes on.** It should look as good at the end of the day as it did at the beginning. Just don't start tidying up when you've got visitors milling around.

- **Use your prospect sheets** and attach them to a clipboard. Store completed sheets in a safe place.

- **Whenever you leave the stand,** take some business cards and promotional material with you. You never know who you may bump into when you're queuing up for a sandwich, so be prepared for business at all times.

- **Make sure that you have reserved space** in your diary for meetings. Again, be organised and ready to offer meetings. Fumbling through your diary for convenient meeting times can appear unprofessional.

- **Keep focused on staying positive throughout the day.** Sometimes this will mean forcing a smile and appearing upbeat even if feeling a little weary. It is a good way to overcome any momentary blues.

Essential Influencing Skills That Really Work

It isn't rare to spend time with a visitor that has a genuine need for your services, to tell them at length how wonderful your business is, to explain how you can help them and for them to still walk away without even a glimmer of a sale. The problem could be that you have been so busy telling them how brilliant you are, that you have overlooked the importance of showing an interest in them.

Before developing my Exhibition Skills workshop I acted as a mystery shopper at many exhibitions. I wanted to find out at first hand how many exhibitors would actually attempt to build a two-way conversation with me, rather than launching a one-sided sales pitch.

The results were surprising.

In the vast majority of cases the person speaking to me was so focused on talking about themselves and their business, that they overlooked the importance of building any rapport with me. In fact, on most occasions when I did eventually pipe up, I would find that my last few words were drowned out as the person dived into the conversation to dominate it once again.

And yet it doesn't take much to make every person that visits your stand feel genuinely pleased that they took a break in their day to find out more about you. It comes down to two things.

- o   Your ability to build genuine rapport
- o   Your body language

Here are a few things that will help build rapport:

- **Be conscious of how you come across** when on your stand.

o Use positive and welcoming body language. The simple act of smiling, nodding and acknowledging what is being said to you is far more important than getting in the first and the last word.

o Adopt an open and welcoming posture and try to make eye contact.

o Wait for an opportunity to speak instead of diving in immediately with a self-introduction. This is so important if the person is enjoying browsing your stand.

o When you do introduce yourself, aim to be friendly and informal. The last thing that somebody wants is a hard nose sales pitch. They will be getting plenty of those from the other exhibitors, so make sure that you stand out by looking for alternative ways to connect.

- **Have some useful 'conversation starters'** when it is clear that you do need to take the lead. Open questions can start a dialogue quite easily. For example:

o "So what has brought you here today?"

o "How many exhibitions do you attend?"

o "What seminars are you attending?"

o "What do you do for a living?"

o " Is there anything in particular that you are looking for today?"

- **Always be thoughtful and courteous.** The person that you are speaking to may not be a potential client but they are visiting your stand so deserve courtesy and consideration. They may well recommend your stand to others but are unlikely to do so if treated a little dismissively.

- **Develop a fantastic capsule introduction.** You only have a few seconds to engage your visitor before their mind starts to wander. Make it easy for every person that approaches your stand to understand exactly what you do. You haven't got long to get to know them, probably only five minutes, so it's important to use that time wisely. Try to encapsulate the following in your introduction:

  o Your name and your business name.

  o Summarise the services and products that you offer in two or three sentences.

  o Explain the types of clients that you work with. Don't reel off a huge list. Inspire them with one or two great case studies that show what you have achieved for similar clients.

  o Now, over to them. Turn the conversation around and start finding out what their need is. What are they looking for? What has brought them to your stand? Who else are they talking to? How can you help them?

- **Demonstrate genuine enthusiasm.** If you can't be enthusiastic about your business then you cannot expect to enthuse your visitor. However, whilst it is easy for us to be enthusiastic about what we are saying, we don't always show the same enthusiasm when listening. Ask questions to demonstrate interest and in doing so you will encourage your visitor to open up. We cover building rapport and influencing skills in more detail in Chapters 2 and 3.

The Importance of Doing Your Sums Afterwards

You've had plenty of visitors and the organisers are now encouraging you to rebook for next year with the promise of a discount, a better stand or a speaker slot. Maybe even all three. It's tempting to say yes, but don't be swept away with this feel good factor. Decline the opportunity to rebook until you have taken stock and done your sums.

o It's vital that you track the value of the business that you have gained from each exhibition and that you contrast this with the expense of exhibiting. Successful marketing on a shoestring is about getting the most from your marketing on a slender budget. This means reviewing your expenses and return every time before committing to the same activity again.

o Realistically, you may not see an immediate return on your spend following an exhibition. It can be many weeks or even months before an enquiry turns into a sale. Keep a record of the new business that you gain as a direct result of the exhibition. It may also be interesting to identify whether the new business came from an existing or lapsed client, a cold or warm prospect.

Should you then decide to exhibit again, you are doing so because you know that making a decent profit is a strong possibility based on your previous experiences and your robust calculations!

Exhibition Checklist

Exhibition date:
Exhibition name:
Exhibitor contact details:

Activity	Yes / No	Notes
Stand booked?		
Lighting / electrical arranged?		
Furniture booked?		
Entry time confirmed?		
Parking confirmed?		
Invitations received?		
Badges/passes delivered?		
Pop-up banner ordered?		
Fabric purchased?		
Stand props arranged?		

Items to Take on the Day	Done ?
Box to store prospect sheets	
Desktop diary	
Pens/staple/folders	
Clipboards	
Corporate clothing	
Promotional gifts	
Stand props	
Display boxes	
Business card and leaflet dispensers	
Business cards	
Marketing materials	
Envelopes	
Name badges	
Sticky tape	

Enquiry Form

Spoken to by:

Full name:

Business name:

Contact details:

Permission given to follow-up by telephone	Y / N
Permission given to follow-up by e-mail	Y / N

Details of conversation:

Meeting booked in diary?

Marketing Materials Issued:

Action to be taken and by whom?

7 HOLD THE FRONT PAGE! HOW TO WIN WITH PR

It's the Holy Grail for small businesses -getting relevant, meaningful and targeted exposure in magazines and newspapers. Yet for many, how to gain PR coverage is a mystery. The odd photograph in the local press celebrating their latest fund-raising initiative is the extent of their activities. Little else is achieved. PR remains a wishful afterthought, the preserve of large organisations with big budgets and a PR agency to broadcast their achievements.

The good news is that PR on a shoestring is within the grasp of *any* small business. The purpose of this chapter is to show you on a step-by-step basis how to achieve great media coverage.

You don't have to be a PR guru, a Chartered Marketer or have dozens of media contacts dangling at your fingertips to get PR coverage on a small budget. In the last 24 years I have met many editors and journalists and often asked what they look for in a press release, what captures their interest and what irritates them! I would like you to regard this chapter as your one-to-one PR seminar. In it, we will discuss what steps you can take to promote your business successfully in the media. You won't need a big budget, but as always you will need to invest your time and energy if you want to be successful. We will cover the following topics in detail:

- The 7 small business benefits of PR
- The 7 deadly PR sins
- Establishing objectives
- 8 creative approaches

- 10 top tips on writing a press release
- Writing an online press release
- How to identify the right publications for your business
- 10 ways to communicate with the media
- How and why you should write a vanity press release
- How to pitch and then present on live radio
- The pulling power of public speaking
- How to increase your sales with PR coverage

The 7 Small Business Benefits of PR

With a little PR know-how plus some passion and persistence your business can really benefit from PR. How?

- **More sales at a low acquisition cost.** Don't let anyone tell you that PR does not lead to sales. It does because it leads to potential clients beating a path to your door to find out more about your business. Because you're investing your time and energy (and not your budget) to get PR coverage, you're acquiring this new business at a very low acquisition cost. Whatever it is that you do for a living, relevant and targeted PR coverage will increase your sales. There is no doubt about it.

- **You'll convert prospective clients in a shorter time frame.** They have already read about you and they're already interested in doing business with you, and yet they haven't even spoken to you. This means that they will make the decision to do business with you in a shorter timescale than if *you* had approached *them*.

- **You are seen as an expert, a market leader in your sector and someone that people refer to in glowing terms.** If you are gaining column inches on a regular basis, sharing your expertise and interesting news, then within a fairly short period of time people will start to think of you as a business person of standing and integrity. Your name will be the one offered when the question is asked, "Do you know anyone who does…?" In a competitive marketplace, this has obvious advantages for your business. Your media coverage will have helped hugely in building a strong reputation.

- **Your actual business is seen as the best in your sector.** If the achievements of your business are being covered in the media on a regular basis, it doesn't take long before people start to regard your business as the market leader and you as an expert. Consequently, your business will attract talented people who are interested in working with you, working for you, or doing business with you.

- **You feel fantastic!** Never underestimate the positive energy that comes with feeling good. If you're getting good quality, regular coverage in the media, whether the coverage focuses on you personally, your business or a mixture of both, you can't help but feel popular and successful. This will have a positive effect on your business dealings and in your personal relationships. You will find yourself on the receiving end of exciting personal and business opportunities that would never have come your way without the power of PR.

- **Your marketing communications become** infinitely more powerful and effective. If you use newsletters, sales letters, brochures, catalogues, flyers or a website to promote your business, then including your PR coverage in each one will massively increase their impact. Rather than telling prospective clients why you are so good at what you do, you can let your coverage in the media do this instead. When words are presented as a news release rather than an advert, your business gains credibility in leaps and bounds. This has real pulling power with cold prospects, warm leads and even your existing clients.

- **The media comes looking for you!** That wonderful day arrives when you are contacted by an editor, a journalist, a television presenter or a radio researcher and they want to know if you would be willing to share your thoughts or insights on a particular subject. Why have they approached you? Because they have read about you themselves, or have been recommended to you by somebody else that has read about you. Don't think that because you're a small-business owner this won't happen to you. If you get to grips with PR then it really is a case of "fasten your seatbelts" and enjoy the ride!

The 7 Deadly PR Sins

Okay, you've sent your press release to the local newspaper and you know that they are always on the look out for business news. Several weeks down the line and they still haven't printed it. You're none the wiser and they are not returning your calls. You're not alone, this scenario is being replayed the length and breadth of the UK with thousands of small businesses. Here are the seven key reasons why most of these press releases end up in the wastepaper bin:

- **Instead of being to the point and newsworthy,** the press release is a rambling block of text. An editor or journalist will simply switch off before they've even got halfway through it. Given that an editor can receive an endless stream of press releases every single day, you can understand why so many are discarded after only a cursory glance.

- **The press release is full of spelling mistakes** and clumsy grammar. Most editors and journalists have spent years developing their written skills. Such releases irritate them enormously and are invariably dismissed.

- **The press release is e-mailed without** any conversation beforehand or follow up afterwards. It sinks into the group of invisible press releases. There are plenty of other people getting on the phone and actually pitching the content of their release to the journalist or editor. If the press release is not sold to an editor or journalist, then it is unlikely to be published.

- **The press release is not actually a press release.** It is an advert dressed up as a press release. Rather than communicating news or something of genuine interest to the readers, it's focused on trying to sell services. The chances are it will be forwarded to the advertising department who will then be chasing you to buy space from them.

- **The press release is brilliant**! It's got a great story, it reads well and it's focused on news. However the content is not relevant so it will not therefore be considered for publication.

- **The press release is sent but no** one has checked on the all-important deadlines when news articles and releases must be submitted. The copy deadline is missed and the press release sinks to the bottom of the pile.

- **The business owner is far too modest!** For many small business owners, blowing their own trumpet and communicating business achievements and positive stories is too much like boasting. Because of this, most of the newsworthy stories that a journalist or editor would love to get their hands on never actually reach them.

You don't have to make any of these mistakes!

Establishing Objectives

Most small businesses want to know how to write press releases that are actually published. In my experience, their main PR focus is on gaining coverage in magazines and newspapers. Press releases, however, are only one part of the PR story. Small businesses that are successful in getting long-term PR coverage don't put all their eggs in one basket. With this in mind we are going to look at:

o Creative ways to gain coverage in magazines, newspapers and journals.
o Opportunities to speak on live radio
o Public speaking at exhibitions, networking events and seminars

Before you write your next great news story or plan your next talk, as always it pays to spend some of your time planning. As a small business with a full agenda, your time is precious. You can't afford to spend it on a marketing activity simply because you think it's a good idea and nothing more. With PR, as with any other marketing approach, it's important that you think through your reasons for embarking on the activity, establishing tangible and compelling objectives.

So, what are the objectives of PR?

Have a look at some of the objectives that delegates from my PR workshops have identified. Are any relevant to yourself?

- o "I want to use PR to build awareness of me and my business. I want PR to help me to stand out from other business coaches that on the face of it look very similar to me even though I am better qualified in the vast majority of cases. I don't like cold calling so I will put my energies into creating top tips articles and columns in magazines in the hope that I will attract potential clients."

- o "We are a small family run business and because we are based in a unit in the middle of the countryside, I want PR to build awareness of our business so that we become more visible. If we are getting regular coverage, it should be easier for me to close sales. If a prospect has found out about us through an article in the local newspaper, the chances are they will not be going elsewhere for a quote."

- o "I want to increase the online sales of my walking and hiking range of products through generating higher levels of awareness both of me and my business with hikers and travellers. I want to contribute to magazines, online forums and blogs where I can build a reputation as a person that shares useful travel tips and travel experiences."

- o "I want to let potential clients know that after spending 15 years working for a large business, I have established my own limited company and I am now offering high value fixed fee bookkeeping services to small businesses."

How you achieve your objectives is an entirely different matter altogether and it's something that we are going to tackle later in the chapter. The most important thing is to sit down and really think through exactly what you want PR to do for your business. Commit your objectives in writing. Don't worry about making these objectives measurable with sales figures. It is difficult, if not impossible to say exactly how much business you want PR to generate or how much awareness you are aiming for. If you do try to guess how much business you will get from PR, the figures you come up with may turn out to be wildly optimistic and you are likely to become disillusioned when you don't reach them. A much better idea instead is to make the objectives measurable but based on the amount of PR coverage that you are aiming for. For example, you could set a PR objective of having your news and articles published in at least three publications in the next six months. You could set an objective of writing and releasing one online press release every single month. You could set another objective of securing a public speaking slot at three events.

Objectives are meaningful when grounded in reality rather than flights of fantasy. And successful PR begins with clear objectives.

How can you achieve your objectives? It's time to pull out the flip chart and get creative.

8 Creative Approaches

Without a doubt, powerful press releases occupy thousands of column inches every single day of the week across a variety of publications - both online and offline. They are a popular and proven way of securing coverage. Journalists and editors alike welcome a well-written, timely and relevant press release. However press releases are not the only way to gain media coverage and if you focus your efforts on these alone and exclude other creative approaches, you'll be missing out on many other opportunities to manoeuvre your business under the media spotlight.

So, although we are going to look in detail at how to write and submit press releases later in the chapter, we will start by looking at other effective and creative approaches that can be used to get your work published.

- **News about you.** This can be a short newsflash or a longer article where you are communicating something of genuine interest about yourself. Remember, as we said earlier, modesty gets you nowhere, so if you've had a dramatic or interesting change of career, for example you have moved from a well-paid, secure and high profile position to starting your own delicatessen or cleaning business, this is newsworthy and could make for a great article. Have you won a prize, or recently qualified in your profession?

  Have you overcome a big hurdle to get to where you are in your business? For example, one of the PR angles I am taking to promote this book is the fact that I have chronic repetitive strain injury in my upper body which means that I cannot physically write or type. I dictate my words using voice recognition software. My headline news is that I am "*The Woman Who Wrote a Book Without Writing a Word*".

  Have you recently landed a fantastic project that you gained as the result of an unconventional approach? (You made a barefaced pitch to the CEO and bypassed all the usual processes. Or, you beat off stiff competition from much larger businesses and won on pure talent)

What made you start your business? Often, what makes you interesting from the media's point of view is not what you do but what inspired you to do it. When you next pick up a magazine or a newspaper, look out for the inspirational stories published about business people and you will see this in practice. There is a great piece of news about you that is just waiting to come out!

- **News about your business and your team**. Again, magazines, newspapers and journals are always interested in genuine, even quirky articles and short news pieces about something that is happening in your business, or with the people that you employ. For example, have you recently downsized your business despite making record profits? Do you operate a very successful business from home with a virtual team? Have you recently launched products and services that are very topical - environmentally friendly or with a local emphasis? Has your team achieved a record-breaking feat? Has your business done something amazing for a local or national charity? If the general economic outlook is gloomy, are you bucking the trend with astonishing sales figures? Once you start thinking, you don't have to look far to find interesting stories.

- **Within you is a guru**! Are you willing to share your views, your knowledge and experience -without trying to sell? Most of us can impart valuable knowledge and in doing so benefit many people. The printed word is a great way of communicating your expertise. Often, what holds us back is the fact that we don't really see ourselves in this light. Take a look at most publications and you will find numerous columns, commentaries, insights and feedback all provided by people who've stepped outside of their comfort zone and dared to call themselves an expert. Why can't you? An article of just 200 words can create a very powerful impression of you. Or how about a column of 150 words?

- **Top tips.** Journalists and editors love articles that focus on dispensing a wealth of valuable information in a compact, easy to read format, otherwise known as top tips. I have managed to secure thousands of column inches for my own business and clients' businesses with top tips articles, and their popularity shows no sign of declining. Whilst the content of top tips articles still involves sharing your expert views, the layout is very different. Here are some top tips formats that I have used in the past:

  - o   5 top tips
  - o   How to....... in 6 easy steps
  - o   3 of the best...
  - o   The number 1 top tip
  - o   4 ways to.......
  - o   Six simple ways to...
  - o   The 7 secrets of

So take a moment to consider whether you would be able to dispense advice in such a format.

A designer wanting to promote his capabilities using the top tips format for example could consider writing one of the following:

- o   5 top tips to promote your business using your business cards
- o   How to brief your design agency in 6 easy steps
- o   3 of the best ways to use your next newsletter as a marketing tool
- o   The number 1 top tip – making your investment in design pay for itself
- o   The 7 secrets of successful sales flyers

Or how about an accountant wanting to promote their services using the top tips formats:

o The 7 secrets that will help reduce your accountancy bill
o 3 of the best book-keeping tips you will ever find
o How to get your invoices paid in 6 easy steps
o The number 1 top tip on how to gain the maximum value from your accountant
o 10 top tips to successfully manage business cash flow

The great thing about writing top tips is that you don't have to be an accomplished writer. You simply need a brief introduction to get things going, for example:

" Joe Bloggs of prize-winning Yorkshire based design agency JBG Creative shares six proven tips on how you can brief your design agency."

Or how about:

"In this article, John Smith of AB Accountancy shares 3 simple bookkeeping tips guaranteed to save you time and money."

Once you've established a simple introduction, you then need to follow through with your tips. Number each tip and decide on the opening sentence for each one before going into more detail on the tip itself. Until you have actually secured a top tips article with a publication, I would not recommend that you spend hours on writing top tips articles. Prepare a good outline instead so that you can discuss it with a publication that is interested in your ideas.

For some general guidance on how to write top tips ... here are some tips!

o   Aim for approximately 500 words on one side of A4 paper. Once you've got your introduction sorted out, which, as you can see from the previous examples can be around 30 words or so, aim to divide your tips with an equal amount of words. For example, if you have five tips then allocate about 90 words per tip. Allow 20 words at the end for a mini biography so you can tell the reader who you are. Make sure that you include any qualifications and recent achievements and don't forget your contact details. As you become more confident with your writing, you can allow yourself more creative freedom. If you have half a page of A4, then you should aim to write around 300 words, following the same principles.

o   You don't have to write long and flowing sentences. The beauty of writing top tips is that you can write short snappy sentences that are much easier to read.

o   Don't worry if you don't think you have enough interesting information to cover 10 tips, aim for 5 or even 3 tips instead.

o   On the other hand, you may have plenty to share. If so, think about spreading your tips over several articles. It's much better to get 3 articles published over 3 months sharing 3 or 4 tips per article, than it is to get just one article published with 10 tips. I often write my top tips articles as part of a series of 3, sharing tips on one subject before moving on to a fresh topic three articles later. The advantage of this approach is that you gain prolonged coverage for your business and along the way you're building a strong relationship with the journalist or editor that has commissioned you.

So hopefully by now you are convinced of the power of top tips. It's time now to turn our attention to the four remaining creative tips.

- **Reviews**. Flick through any magazine or newspaper, or visit a website or forum and you are likely to come across reviews. So, what can *you* review? How about a supplier's improved product or service? A customer's brand new product or service? A relaunched website that is asking visitors to give feedback on the new content and layout? A training facility that is aimed at your sector? An exhibition organiser requesting written feedback from visitors and exhibitors? The beauty of PR is that it has a viral effect and something as simple as reviewing a product could attract the attention of a journalist reading the reviews. Bear this in mind when submitting your reviews, making sure they are well composed and insightful.

- **A joint client case study.** If you are a small business that attracts big clients, then a joint client case study with one of these clients can be an easy way to attract column inches. However, the media is not interested in the fact that you have a big client. They want to know what you are doing with this client that makes your case study newsworthy. So, if you have delivered something out of the ordinary for your client or you have developed an innovative or groundbreaking product or service, these initiatives will usually be regarded as newsworthy. The most important thing is that you enlist the co-operation of your client so that together you can build a powerful case study. I would not recommend you spend hours slaving over a word-perfect case study. Sketch out your idea so that you can talk it through with a journalist. They may want to write your case study themselves rather than work from something that you have already written.

- **Charity/Fundraiser.** If you are doing great things to help your community you should be telling your local newspapers and business magazines about it. The amount of coverage will not usually extend to many column inches and it tends to be image based - a nice photograph with a few lines of accompanying text - but these articles do serve to build a really positive impression of your small business for the readers.

- **Entering and winning awards.** This is another way to gain column inches and build your profile as an expert in your sector at the same time. If you're not confident of winning a national award, why not enter a local business award? You may not win but the media coverage will put you in the spotlight. How do you find out about awards? Start reading your local newspapers and business magazines intently and ask your Chamber of Commerce if they launch annual business awards.

Hopefully, your head is now buzzing with ideas. Having looked at these creative approaches, it is time now to think of 2 or 3 that appeal to you. Explore your ideas in more detail over the coming weeks. With PR, the more creative you can be with your ideas, the better. The desks of editors and journalists are heavy with lacklustre and boring articles and press releases. Sketch your initial thoughts on a flip chart or whiteboard and start to pad them out.

When you start talking to journalists and editors (something that we are covering in detail later on) you must inspire them with your ideas and enthusiasm. You have to feel inspired yourself so if you struggle creatively when working ask people to work with you and reward them with food and drink after your creative brainstorming. It will probably turn out to be a successful exercise and a lot of fun too.

10 Top Tips on Writing Press Releases

Here I am with the top tips again, but they are effective for communicating information in a simple and concise format. There is definitely an art to writing press releases and getting them published. The good news is that if you spend a little time polishing up your skills and follow these tips, you will be rewarded with your work in print.

- **Get the basic layout of your press release right**. Study and then follow the layout of any of the press release examples at the end of this chapter and you won't go wrong. They follow a fairly standard approach that is recognised by journalists and editors.

- **Find a hook.** We also covered this earlier when we were looking at writing interesting articles. Every good press release has an interesting angle, whether you are communicating a message about your business that is topical within your sector, you have gained an accreditation for your business, won an award, secured an incredible deal, or downsized your successful business by moving into a home-based office. If you don't have an interesting angle, then you don't have a genuine press release. Start looking for that angle.

- **Use a strong title headline.** In Chapter 5 there are many tips on how to create great headlines including lots of practical examples. You can apply many of these tips when writing your press release headlines also. If you are after a news style of headline, then you will find inspiration simply from studying the business headlines in the newspapers. They tend to be short and to the point rather than long and elaborate. Keep your press release headline to one line of text. If you can't think of a headline that is catchy or clever, don't worry. Aim for a headline that tells the story of what follows in just a few words. Your headline doesn't have to be gimmicky but it does have to be accurate. And it must be relevant to the text that follows.

- **Include a strong opening paragraph.** This is one of the most important parts of your press release. If the opening paragraph lacks bite, and there is no link with the headline, then you run the risk of the editor or journalist discarding your work. You need to define the one or two compelling messages that your press release hinges upon and focus on these in the first paragraph. If your release is focusing on something that is truly innovative, revolutionary or groundbreaking then the place to communicate this is here. Make sure that your website is mentioned as there is every chance that whilst the journalist or editor is reading your press release, they will scan your website as well. It should take you as long to write your introductory paragraph as it does the rest of your press release. If you can reinforce a point you are making in the opening paragraph with a fact or a statistic, put it in. Keep your release factual. This is a press release and not an advert. Hold back on those superlatives and it will be far more interesting and genuine.

- **Use quotations wherever possible.** You can add real human interest to your press release by illustrating a point you are making with a quote from you or a member of your team. Take a look at the press release examples included at the end of this chapter and you will see that each one includes quotations. Sometimes a journalist or editor will be so impressed with your quotations that they will embolden your best quotation within the news piece that they publish. Make sure, therefore, that the quotations you include are interesting.

- **Keep your press release to one side of A4.** You are not writing a book so focus on communicating the key points. Before anyone actually reads your press release, they are likely to scroll over it. If it looks wordy and long, they may not go any further. So even though it is tempting on occasions to write a lengthy tome, try to restrict it to one side of A4.

- **By all means use bold and italics** when you want to reinforce an important point or highlight an interesting quotation. But resist the temptation to pepper your press release with capital letters, different typefaces and type sizes. Stick to one typeface and one type size only for the body text. It's a good idea to make the headline of your press release larger than the body text so that it grabs attention.

- **Make sure that your press release** is checked before sending it. Whether you are a creative genius or this is your very first attempt, have your release checked with a fine toothcomb. Don't ask for praise or flattery, just for any spelling mistakes, clumsy grammar and typographical errors to be spotted. Does your release flow or falter? As explained earlier, editors love press releases that they can read and simply place into their publication without any further alteration.

- **Include a brief company description.** Your press release should conclude with a short paragraph describing your company and your products and services. If you are writing a joint press release with a partner company or client, include separate descriptions of both companies. Above all, include the name and full contact details of the person that the editor or journalist can contact. But don't attach a high-resolution image of your logo until you have checked with the editor or journalist that they can accept it.

- **Make your accompanying e-mail a mini press release.** It is likely that after picking up the telephone and selling the content of your press release to your media contact, you will be e-mailing it. The e-mail that accompanies your press release should be a mini version of it, in which you highlight the key points. Often, if it is near the publication date when your press release comes in, an editor or journalist won't have time to read it. However, if your e-mail provides a good all-round impression of your press release, it will make it easy for them to revisit your e-mail when things quieten down. Your e-mail should ideally be no more than five or six lines, followed by a few bullet points that focus on the interesting parts.

Writing an Online Press Release

Access the Internet and type in the sentence, " How can I submit online press releases?" and you will be deluged with websites that promise amazing responses to your press release, at no cost. You can actually spend hours going through these websites and walk away with nothing more than cramp in your fingers. That is not to say that posting online press releases is a bad idea. But if a service is billed as completely free, in all likelihood there are thousands of people using that service to post their press releases and it's unlikely that a journalist is going to be able to sift through the content and find yours. In Chapter 8 there are many tips on how you can effectively build your PR presence online through social networking and contributing to forums as an alternative to relying on press releases. If you want to get your press releases published online, then by all means try the free approach, but know when to call it a day.

The two websites that I have used to post online press releases are: *www.sourcewire.com* and *www.responsesource.com*. Both of these websites make a small charge (in the region of £40 plus VAT) for posting your press release, but they are widely used by journalists, editors and PR people looking for news. When you post your press release on either of these two websites, it is also sent out to a list of subscribing journalists, news desks and online publications, relevant to its content. Press releases on these websites get picked up by several news sites which helps drive traffic to your website. What is more, if a reader likes your press release they can submit it to social bookmarking and networking sites including Facebook, Digg and Del.icio.us where it can be rated and commented on by members. That means even more exposure for you!

If you're interested in finding out more about submitting online press releases on either *www.responsesource.com* or *www.sourcewire. com* then speak to one of the team at Daryl Willcox Publishing, (*www.dwpub.com*), the publishing group behind both websites. They will guide you through the process of creating and submitting your online press release and explain the costs to you.

When it comes to actually writing your online press release, the exact same rules apply as for a standard press release. The only difference between the two is that if you want your online press release to generate an increase in online visitors to your website, then you will need to add links to your website within the text. It is also a good idea to include a few of the key words that people use when they are searching for your products or services. By doing this, your online press release will become a signpost that guides interested prospects through to your website.

What you have to remember is that whether people are reading about you on the Web or in a publication, you must create a press release that will make them stop in their tracks and actually read the text.

How to Identify the Right Publications for Your Business

You're now at the stage where you have developed some interesting storylines about your business, you know how to write a press release, and you're cooking up some exciting creative approaches that will promote you and your business in the media.

It's time now to crank your PR plan up a notch by identifying the publications in which you would really like to secure free coverage.

Here is how you go about this:

o   When you are chatting to cold prospects, ask them to tell you what publications they read.

o   Ask your existing clients what publications they read and which ones they prefer. This will give you a feel for the best publications to target.

o   Use the Internet to search for publishing houses and individual publications with titles that you think could reach potential new clients. A few hours on Google can yield some good results.

o Whilst you are on the Internet, look for online publications and newsletters that are aimed at the target audiences you want to reach. Ask your clients and cold prospects if they are regular visitors on any particular websites.

o Visit your local library and ask if they have any lists of magazines and newspapers. You may be lucky or you may draw a blank, but it's worth a visit to find out.

o Find out from your local Chamber of Commerce or Business Link if they can furnish you with any media lists.

o Take a look at the Audit Bureau of Circulations website. (*www.abc.org.uk*) This website includes a useful list of good publishing houses together with the publications that are under their umbrella.

o Now, armed with a list of publications get on the telephone and request both current and back copies of each one you are interested in. At this stage, it will help if you ask for some basic information. Do they have an editorial policy? Who is the person to speak to regarding editorial? Can they give you their forthcoming editorial deadlines? If you are also targeting online publications and you are not given a phone contact, send a nicely composed e-mail asking for the editorial information instead.

o Within a short space of time, you will be deluged with magazines, journals and newspapers. What you do now is absolutely vital if you want to gain targeted, meaningful and free exposure for your business. There are no shortcuts, but your efforts will be well rewarded. In effect you have two choices. You can either flick through each publication before picking up the phone and pitching your idea. If you do this, you may or may not be successful in securing some free coverage. Or, you can turn into a real bookworm with every single publication that has been sent to you. This means reading each publication from cover to cover. Whilst you are reading, start to form opinions on the look, feel and content of the publication. What is the style and focus? How much space is given to editorial rather than advertising? Are there regular columns and features, news pages, business articles, top tips and reviews? Do small business guest writers contribute? This is the time when you have to get under the skin of that publication so that you know it inside out. By doing this you're going to be in a very good position when you pick up the phone and start to pitch your ideas.

○ You now know everything there is to know about the publication, so it's time to ask yourself the pivotal question: *"Where can I add real value to this publication, and how?"*

○ It's as simple as that. If you focus on looking at how you can add value, the chances are that you are going to be greeted with open arms by journalists and editors. But, it doesn't stop there. No time to rest on your laurels. You now move to the next stage - picking up the phone and communicating.

10 Ways to Communicate with the Media

The phone is staring at you and you're ready to make those crucial calls that could lead to the best free exposure that your business has ever had. It's exciting, but it's also nerve racking.

- **It will help significantly if you are well prepared** before the telephone is in your hand. Sketch out your news story or topical ideas. You need to have a beginning, middle and an end in place and this will help you talk through your ideas. Have those enticing and newsworthy bullet points in front of you so that you don't dry up halfway through the conversation. Do you remember all your great ideas for columns and top tips? Now is the time to have those notes in front of you.

- **Don't be afraid to practise your approach** on a friend or colleague. In my early days of negotiating for PR coverage, I would spend ages practising what I wanted to say until I became natural and fluent.

- **Get yourself into a positive and enthusiastic** frame of mind. Now is not the time to play down your proposition or your achievements.

- **Pick up the phone** and ask to speak to the editorial contact. Unfortunately it could be that you have got yourself all psyched up for nothing. In the real world, you won't always get through on a first call, but be patient. It could take several calls before you strike gold or even several e-mails if you don't have the option of phoning.

- **You've got through!** It's time to discuss your great ideas for securing editorial coverage. How do you start? Well, begin by giving a professional introduction. Let the person know that you have a sound idea or some great news that you think will either inspire their readers, or be of real interest to them. At this stage, you are calling to outline your thoughts. Refer back to your earlier research and communicate your appreciation and knowledge of the publication. If you enjoyed a particular article say so. If you found a column really interesting, comment on it. If you really liked the front cover, the back page, the inside spread, the discussion group, the forum, the letters page, tell them. If you are genuine, sincere and specific with your positive feedback this will encourage your contact to listen favourably to your proposition. When the vast majority of business people pitch to the media they spend most of the time talking about themselves and it can turn out to be a short conversation.

- **Establish your credentials** and why you should be in that publication. Gently ease into the conversation the positive points about you and your business. If you've appeared in other publications, if you've recently been on the radio or on the television, if you've got many years of invaluable experience in your sector, let the person know this. Make sure that you gently weave these points into the conversation so you don't sound as if you're boasting.

- **Offer an exclusive to the publication.** If they agree to your ideas, tell them you will not approach any other publication with the same material. Not only is this a good negotiation tactic, it also shows that you are professional in your dealings with the media.

- **Be prepared to listen.** It could be that the person you're talking to embraces your ideas immediately. However, they may like the sound of you and ask you to write an article or submit some tips or news on another subject. Say yes to their proposal if you are happy to run with this. But don't be afraid to say no either. The last thing you want is a headache because you've agreed to write about a subject on which you know absolutely nothing.

- **If you are given the green light**, then it's all stations go and time to discuss the small details. How many words should you write? What's the deadline? To whom should you send your copy and in what format? Obtain answers to each of these questions because you don't want problems to arise at the last-minute.

- **Be enthusiastic,** say thank you and confirm what has been agreed. It's time now to punch the air, shout out loud, and do a small dance or whatever you like to do when celebrating a milestone. Then, compose an e-mail to your media contact, confirming every single detail!

It's now down to you to deliver. My advice is that you put as much, if not more effort into delivering as you did into your preparation and pitching. If you are given 500 words, then write exactly 500 words, not 450 or 750. Aim to get your work to the publication at least three days before the final deadline. After you have sent your work through, pick up the phone and check that it has been received. If it doesn't get published, ask why. When it does get published, get on the phone again and ask for feedback and show your appreciation. Suggest a meeting with your editorial contact to discuss opportunities for appearing in the publication on a regular basis.

Always talk about delivering newsworthy stories and articles to the readers and focus on adding value. Never take your relationship with a publication for granted no matter how frequently they publish your work. You need them much more than they need you. Ensuring that your contact has received your piece and that they are happy with your content is one way of demonstrating your respect for the arrangement.

These small touches make a big difference. On numerous occasions I have secured ongoing free PR coverage by initially submitting a small article or one piece of news. Focus on developing high-value relationships with a small number of publications that are pleased to receive your work. It is these relationships that can blossom, rather than those with publications that are only interested in publishing your work on rare occasions.

If you start to submit articles on a regular basis, make sure that you continue to read the particular publications from cover to cover. Are there any new emerging trends? Can you make further suggestions to improve a publication? It's much easier to go into this territory when you have an existing relationship. It's about building trust through being reliable, respectful and delivering good quality work.

How And Why You Should Write a Vanity Press Release

The vast majority of press releases that are sent to publications by small businesses are in fact vanity releases. Rather than communicating genuine news that readers find interesting, they focus on communicating information that is of little or no interest to readers. You may be thrilled with the fact that you have taken on two new team members, but if there is no hook, and consequently nothing of real value in the story to grab readers, then your release will not get published.

There is a value however in writing a vanity press release provided you have no intention whatsoever of releasing it to any publications. If that sounds a little odd, bear with me for a moment.

One of the biggest marketing challenges a small business faces is how to keep in touch with cold prospects and clients beyond sending out a brochure or a newsletter. What I have found is that communicating news about your business using the format of a press release is very effective.

- **Look upon a vanity press release** as a creative communication that looks like a press release, and that enables you to share news about your business to clients and prospects. You use the same format as for a press release that you send to the media and you spend just as long working on it, but you have a free rein over the content. It doesn't need a hook because it's not being published.

- **Let's say you are planning on attending** an exhibition as an exhibitor. A vanity press release is a great way to communicate key information about your business to visitors. If you look at the example of the vanity press release at the end of this chapter, the business in question, HH Design were exhibiting at a prestigious event and wanted the guests to know that they were responsible for designing the logo and accompanying literature for the organisation hosting the event. Their vanity press release proved to be a good conversation starter with people visiting their stand.

- **If you want to tell customers and prospects** about your move into new premises, that you have a brand new website, that you have launched a new product or service, then presenting this information as a vanity press release is a great way to do this.

So by all means use a vanity press release to make your message stand out, but don't send it to the media! Use it as a direct marketing tool for your customers, warm prospects and cold leads.

How to Pitch and Then Present on Live Radio

So far, we have concentrated on gaining coverage in publications because this is a big area on which to focus and one in which amazing results can be gained. However, don't overlook the importance of appearing on local radio as part of building your PR profile. Local radio stations are often on the look out for interesting business stories and case studies. The secret to making it onto those live airways lies in the quality of your preparation.

- **Identify the local radio stations** that cover the geographic areas where you are looking to do business. This is a straightforward exercise and searching on the Internet, looking in local business directories and tuning in to channels will lead you to the appropriate radio stations. When you've found them, visit their websites. You should find some useful information that will help with your preparation work.

- **Tune in and listen!** Listen for any business slots they broadcast and the type of local news they cover. Do they have programmes where they promote local events, local business people or interesting local businesses? Are any programmes delivered by a local business person? Do they deliver interesting or quirky business news?

- **Follow the same process outlined earlier.** Where can you add value for the station? Why should listeners be interested in your news or your ideas? What are they covering at the moment that will reinforce your proposition?

- **In my experience, local radio stations are always** on the look out for genuine interesting stories and news to spice up their content. So when you've mapped out your news or your story, it's simply a matter of picking up the phone and selling your idea. If you have genuine news, then you will need to speak to the newsroom. If you have an idea for a programme then you will usually need to speak to the researcher. Don't be afraid to ask for a brief meeting to discuss your ideas if you are given a warm reception.

- **If you receive a warm reception** and they agree to you having some live airtime to talk with the presenter and the listeners about an aspect of your business - what do you do next? The devil lies in the detail and your delivery!

  o Don't take a script with you. This will not engage the presenter or the listeners. Instead, compile a sheet of bullet points and make each one stand out, either by highlighting each one in different colours or circling key points. It is easy to get carried away in a radio interview and then realise afterwards that you barely touched upon your key points. Listeners cannot see that you are referencing notes and the presenter won't mind.

  o Dress to impress and always take business cards. It's good to leave a lasting positive impression with the producer and presenter, especially if you want to be invited back.

  o Arrive early so that you can secure a car parking space if one has not already been allocated for you. Aim to get there an hour earlier than needed and find somewhere quiet to run through your notes. Positive self-talk is important at this stage to prevent the nerves from creeping in.

o   Book in with the radio station reception about half an hour beforehand unless you have been given different instructions by the team. Either you will be lucky and will bump into other presenters, or it will simply be a matter of waiting in reception and fighting those butterflies!

o   Run through your expectations of the interview with the presenter before you go on air. Have an informal chat to cover the questions they want to ask and vice versa, and agree the content. Make sure that the presenter knows your name and the name of your business. Ask if they can give you a recorded copy of your interview afterwards.

o   When you are live on air, concentrate on speaking clearly and enthusiastically. Make a conscious effort not to umm and err and be enthusiastic. Don't rush through what you want to say. Focus instead on pausing and emphasising keywords. You will sound confident and listeners will find it easy to understand what you are saying.

o   It's important that when talking, you maintain good eye contact with the presenter. You don't have the luxury of asking in a live situation whether you have said enough or it's time to shut up!

o   If you're allowed to give your contact details, do so very clearly at the end and repeat them for good effect.

o   Thank the presenter when you are off air, pat yourself on the back and ask for that copy of the interview. The fun really begins on the way home when you replay your interview. If you're like me, you will be smiling

211

and groaning in equal measure. There's always room for improvement.

And keep listening to those radio stations. Once you have appeared on live radio and done a good job, you could well be invited back and any further ideas you have will be given a fair hearing.

The Pulling Power of Public Speaking

Public speaking is another great vehicle to help build your profile. It is generally acknowledged that most business people don't enjoy public speaking, so if you are willing to give it a good go, you're unlikely to encounter competitors vying for the same opportunities. Entire books have been devoted to the subject of public speaking so if you're serious about presenting in public, start reading and get practising. Why not join a local speaking group or a Toastmasters group? When you feel confident enough to put yourself out there as a public speaker, start by identifying local opportunities to speak. It's usually a good idea to start with small and sympathetic audiences before you tackle the national venues. How about

o Finding out if there are speaker slots or seminar slots at local and regional exhibitions, business conferences and business seminars?

o Volunteering to take on the longer speaking slots when they are offered at your networking group and offering to speak at ad hoc networking events?

o Offering to speak at business events where the organisers may not have considered using a speaker before? They may agree that it will add some extra sparkle to their programme. Don't be afraid to suggest this.

o Researching the speaking opportunities with local interest groups, and the Women's Institute?

o When you're feeling more ambitious, reviewing the business exhibitions that are held throughout the United Kingdom? (make sure that the profile of visitor is compatible with the profile of new clients that you hope to attract.) Don't assume that a large exhibition will automatically have a line up of great speakers and that there is no point approaching the organisers. Often, there are opportunities for charismatic small-business owners to speak at the seminars that run alongside the keynote speaker programme.

Don't pitch! Entertain and inspire instead

If you are using public speaking to raise the profile of your business, then it's not a good idea to fill your speaking slot with a thinly disguised sales pitch. People that pitch and sell when given a platform to entertain do not usually generate positive PR for their business. Focus instead on giving and sharing your expertise or perhaps talk about your business experiences in general. If you have overcome setbacks or barriers, then sharing these in a positive manner can win you the respect of your audience. People will be talking about you in glowing terms long after the event has ended. Sharing useful business insights will also make you an attractive proposition to an event organiser looking for something just that bit different. Always aim to share and give as much as possible.

Increase your impact with the power of the written word

When you are invited to speak, it's likely there will be some pre-event publicity to raise the profile of the event and encourage sell-out attendance. If you are speaking and the event is being publicised with a programme, make sure that you're in it. This is your opportunity to have your details circulated to a wide audience and to get your name in print. Ask how many words the event organisers would like you to contribute to the programme and the type of content that they are looking for.

Some organisers will ask for your biography and they will use it as the basis of a description about you. It should ideally be no more than two or three paragraphs in length, comprising of a brief summary of your experience, your qualifications and achievements, and what you are doing now.

You may be asked to write a few words on the content of your talk instead. Once you have confirmed how many words you can write, start to think about what will really motivate people to come and listen to you.

o It will help the audience if they are given some useful information about you and what qualifies you to stand in front of them and dispense your wisdom.

o They will also want to know what you're going to be talking about and how they will benefit from listening to you.

o You have to make this 'mini article' a real call to action to fill all those seats. Once you have built a reputation as an entertaining, inspiring and motivational public speaker, you will find yourself in big demand!

As an example, here is what I provided to promote a PR talk at a recent business event.

"When it comes to achieving PR On a Shoestring, award-winning Chartered Marketer Dee Blick is in a league of her own. In the last 12 months alone, she has managed to secure over £100,000 of free

media coverage for herself and her clients. Dee has also won three advertising and PR awards from two national magazines, her articles and press releases generating the highest reader responses in a 12-month period. In June of this year, Dee was approached by the BBC and asked to appear in Beat The Boss as a marketing entrepreneur. This involved 3 1/2 days of filming on location and at Dee's home. Bring your notebook because in this informal and lively 40 minute PR master class, Dee will share with you how exactly you can develop a practical PR plan for your business, the most effective ways in which you can communicate with editors and how you can deliver genuinely interesting and compelling news, articles and tips. She will use real-life up-to-the-minute case studies to give the talk some bite and to make it relevant. Dee will stay behind afterwards to answer all your questions."

This probably sounds a little over the top, but remember you are in effect selling the talk and so trying to make it appeal to as many people as possible.

Another benefit of public speaking is that it often leads to substantial local media coverage for which you have had to do nothing other than stand up and speak. Most events are covered in local newspapers and magazines and the speaker line up and programme always gets attention and coverage.

So, exercise those vocal chords on a public platform and you never know where they may take you!

How to Increase Your Sales with PR Coverage

It's a fantastic feeling when you see your name in print, accompanied by a generous amount of text that you played a part in creating. You can of course just stop at this, admire your coverage and hope that readers will be beating a path to your door. This does happen.

However, in my experience, if you really want to get the most from your PR coverage then it pays to make every single column inch that you have gained work really hard for you. This means getting on your soapbox or if you prefer, getting out your foghorn and telling the world that you have arrived!

Here are some cost free ways to do this:

- **When networking**, whether chatting online or at your local networking group, make sure that the people you are networking with know where you are featuring. As we discussed earlier, if people know how well you are doing they will be recommending you when suitable opportunities arise.

- **What about your website?** Do you have a news page on it where you keep visitors updated regularly? If so, use this page to post updates on your media coverage. Why not include copies of your articles and press releases? I do this myself via my own website and it is an effective way of letting people know that you are making waves in the media.

- **When sending out e-mails**, why not add a footer message that alerts the recipient to your PR coverage? Something along the lines of "Look out for Our Column in …." or, "To See Our Latest Media Coverage Go to Our Website" is enough. Don't worry if the people reading these messages are not necessarily the people that you want to target for new business. It's costing you nothing and you could emerge with a new client from the most unexpected quarters. Remember, good news spreads but it's down to you to communicate it.

- **When creating your direct mail letters**, newsletters and flyers consider including snapshots of your media coverage. Again, it costs nothing other than your time and by communicating your media coverage you are building a very positive impression of your business with both cold prospects and existing clients. Don't underestimate the power of PR where your existing clients are concerned. You will gain further respect in their eyes when made aware of your growing media presence and it makes recommendations even easier.

- **If you have an exhibition coming up**, make sure that you place some copies of the publications on your stand or perhaps go further and produce a document that provides an overview of your PR coverage.

- **When you are on the telephone** trying to open doors with cold prospects you can move the conversation to a more positive level simply by discussing your feature or article in a publication that they may have read. Asking if they have read the latest issue is a good way to break the ice.

So, I hope that by now you are encouraged to begin your PR on a shoestring campaign. You can do it! And if you need any motivation to start, just think of those extra sales that will come your way in exchange for your time, persistence and creativity.

Press Release - For Immediate Release

Breadstop Launch "Soggy Sandwich" Survey

Hot on the heels of their immensely popular "Cheerio to the chiller cabinet sandwich" campaign, aimed at consumers, Lingfield based Breadstop (*www.breadstop.co.uk*) are launching a "Soggy Sandwich" survey aimed at businesses that order sandwich platters.

Said Kate Taylor Smith, Director of Breadstop, "We are using this light-hearted survey to highlight a more serious issue which is that for many organisations, when it comes to ordering sandwich platters, neither health nor nutrition are high on their agenda. Often, many platters are delivered in un-refrigerated vans and the sandwiches have been made at such an early hour in the day, or even the night before, that they are past their best. *In a worst-case scenario they can even pose a threat to health.*"

Part of the "Soggy Sandwich" Survey entails finding out how businesses are catering for clients and if they do their bit for the environment by ordering locally. Continues Kate, "What we have seen in recent months is a steady growth in our sandwich platter business from organisations that want to know where their food has come from and how it has been prepared. We only work with local suppliers so we can tell our clients exactly how many food miles has gone into their platter. We also make our sandwiches in the most delicious additive free locally baked bread. We collect the sandwich platters and reuse them, unlike the silver platters that go into landfill."

Breadstop are offering a free sandwich in exchange for completion of the survey. "It will only take a few minutes to complete and we're even paying for the postage. Once we get the survey back, we will contact the business and deliver one of our delicious sandwiches free of charge. We are confident that our sandwiches are the best. They certainly beat the soggy, tasteless sandwiches that have been adorning platters for too long," concludes Kate.

Ends

Press Release - For Immediate Release

It's Time to Stop Smoking Pipes

For decades, plumbers and builders have relied upon hot soldering to join pipes together. It's a process with many disadvantages including scorched skirting boards, burnt fingers, and the need for a heat permit with an obligatory two-hour stay afterwards. There is also the thorny subject of energy conservation and the growing need for the construction sector to embrace energy conserving strategies and products.

Just-For-Copper, (*www.solderlesscopperbonding.com*) is an innovative product that provides a safe and tested alternative to hot soldering. WRAS approved, it permanently joins rigid copper pipes and fittings in minutes without the need for hot soldering. It saves energy and time and is rated at 500 PSI on rigid copper pipes of 25 mm. It is a chemical weld that comes in a trade size bottle. It will be demonstrated at Interbuild, October 2007 Stand A141 Hall 4.

Says Mike Schlup, Managing Director of Kalimex Ltd, the sole UK importers of Just-for-Copper, "This product has been a bestseller in America for many years. The first thing that we did when we brought it into the UK was to certify it with the Water Regulatory Advisory Service (WRAS) to BS6920. It has also undergone a series of independent safety and performance tests. Just-For-Copper is now being distributed UK wide through builders and plumbers merchants."

Concludes Schlup "At Interbuild we will be running live demonstrations and encouraging both visitors and journalists to put Just-For-Copper to the test. It's my firm belief that within the next three years this product will be in every single builder and plumber's tool kit. It's not just a product for now, it's a product for the future."

Ends

(Example Vanity Release)

Press Release - For Immediate Release

HH Design Celebrate Paritas Launch at Ropetackle

Gatwick based HH Design are celebrating the launch of Paritas. Responsible for developing and designing the stunning and vibrant Paritas identity, the HH Design team were awarded the project by unanimous vote. Said Graham Laker, Managing Director, "This project was a real joy for every member in our team. It really helped that we were given a thorough written and verbal brief from the West Sussex Works project team. After many line drawings, mood boards and team discussions, we arrived at a design that embraces colourful, warm and vibrant imagery, plus an open and accessible typeface that links beautifully to the strap line. For some people, the imagery represents flowers and nature, for others it's a butterfly or simply an exquisite collection of shapes. That's the beauty behind design of this nature – it's open to positive interpretation."

HH Design has also designed and built the new Paritas website, www. paritas.org.uk, plus a range of striking pop-up exhibition banners, letterheads, business cards, folders and compliment slips.

So far, the response has been extremely positive. Said David Cain, Paritas project manager, "HH Design have exceeded our expectations and played a key part in building this exciting project."

HH Design are now looking to broaden their public sector client base so that they can deliver more stunning creative work - work that turns heads and most importantly that gets results.

Ends

8 E-MARKETING GEMS FOR NON-TECHNICAL PEOPLE,
by Gareth Sear

E-marketing is a massive topic and many books have been written exploring it. As a small-business owner, where do you start? What are the right tools that you can apply to develop your own successful online marketing strategy without spending a fortune? What follows are some really simple and proven tips that I have used with success to market and promote my business on a small budget using the power of the World Wide Web. There are also some e-marketing tactics in this chapter that I don't fully use but even so, they're worth bringing to your attention so you can consider them.

I started out with little knowledge of e-marketing and found my way through reading, research and trial and error. One of the challenges of developing a programme of e-marketing tactics is having enough time and I wouldn't recommend you try and tackle everything in this chapter immediately. Start by looking at one or two things that you can get your teeth into and get these up and running before moving onto other areas that capture your interest. You will find tips that can be put into practice immediately, where all you need do is follow the instructions. With other tips it's likely that you will need to explore the subject in more detail by talking to your web developer. So, what are we going to cover? Here goes!

- E-mail newsletters
- Search engines
- Google Page Rank

- Search Engine Optimisation
- Links
- Directories
- Forums
- Articles
- Web 2
- Pay per click advertising

E-mail newsletters

An e-mail newsletter is a simple marketing communications tool that enables you to reach customers and prospects quickly, easily and with a small budget. You have probably received hundreds of e-mail newsletters over the years and deleted the vast majority without even looking at the contents. However they can work, if you set time aside to develop a newsletter that is good enough to read. Here are five benefits of e-mail newsletters.

o   With the right content, they can be relevant and interesting communications that you send on a regular basis, to keep your existing customers loyal and interested. At the same time, you can use them to get the attention of prospects that are interested in finding out more about your products and services. These will often be the people that have visited your website and signed up to receive your newsletter.

o   You can alert your customers to any new products or services within a few hours of making your decision to do so.

o   You can motivate customers and prospects alike to contact you by communicating any special offers in the pipeline.

o   You can remind your customers that you are still around and that you care about them.

    o   You can share advice and information that your customers would regard as useful.

I send regular e-mail newsletters for all of these reasons. The Internet is a fickle place with customers having an endless range of businesses to choose from, all in the comfort of their own home or their office. Imagine one street with a thousand businesses selling similar products to you. This is great for customer choice and great for a bargain. However, it's not so great for making you stand out. You have to be at the front of your customers' minds when they are in the market to buy. This is where your e-mail newsletter can really help. It's likely that you've always given your customers impeccable service, which in most cases is reason enough for them to come back. But in a world that is becoming more price conscious and where customers are increasingly shopping around, not only do they demand good service, they want to know they're getting the best value. By using an e-mail newsletter to keep in touch with them, you're helping to build on their loyalty and maintain their interest so they don't go elsewhere.

Who should your newsletter be aimed at?

This needs to tie in with your sales objectives. Referring back to Chapter 1 where you defined your target audiences, you may have several groups that you want to aim your newsletter at, including your existing customers. Each group will respond to a different message and this needs to be reflected in the content of your newsletter. For example, you don't want to be talking about your new banner printing service when prospects are interested in your marketing consultancy services. Using your marketing plan to guide you, decide on the different groups that you want your newsletter to be aimed at.

What should your newsletter include?

On your website you should have plenty of information rich content that you want people to know about including:

o Newsworthy items - stories about your business, or your sector in general that people would be interested in reading
o Testimonials or references from delighted customers
o New products or services
o Press releases
o Special offers

These are all good starting points for planning the content for your newsletter. Get that flip chart out again and think about genuinely interesting news and offers that you can include. How about including a competition or a brief survey, asking customers for their feedback? If you need more inspiration, go back to Chapter 4 where there are many tips on how to write a printed newsletter. These tips can be applied to your e-mail newsletter too.

So how can you create and send an e-mail newsletter?

First things first, you need to have the e-mail contact details of the people that you want to e-mail - usually your customers and potential customers. You also need to have their permission to e-mail before you start sending your newsletter. Once you have your list, it's time to start looking for software that will enable you to create and send your newsletter. There are many software packages available. I use one called Pure360, (*www.pure360.com*) where I currently pay £50 to send 2000 newsletters each month. The system is highly regarded with many useful features that you should look for when choosing a software package. These include:

o An excellent statistics package so you can see who has clicked on to what link, who has opened the newsletter, who has sent it to a friend and more. These statistics can help you refine what you offer to different groups, so your newsletters become even more targeted and relevant.

o A link where recipients can e-mail the newsletter to a friend.

o The option for you to send a text only newsletter at the same time as a graphics based newsletter. This is useful as some people have their e-mail set up to receive text-based messages only.

o The option for you to have different titles so you can analyse which one works best.

You also get a huge amount of support from their customer service team, which is something that I have found invaluable.

One of my friends sends his e-mail newsletters using a system called Joomla and e-mail newsletter software called Acajoom. Referred to as open source software, this software is free to download from the Internet and generally free to use. Although open source software is free, you may need a good understanding of computer software packages to use it. It is also a good idea to have a chat with your web developer to see if an e-mail newsletter software package is already attached to your website.

Spam (No, not the meat in a tin!)

Spam is classed as unwanted e-mails. Some e-mail programmes are set to automatically put certain e-mails in 'junk' or Spam folders - not a good place to be. You don't want your newsletter ending up in junk, as it may never be opened. Some Spam filters will automatically send your e-mail back to you. They will scan your e-mail for certain words or images and if it doesn't pass a number of rules it won't get through to the person you sent it to. I recently found out that using the word 'free' in your e-mail can cause this to happen, as many e-mails classed as Spam offer 'free' things. To prevent this from happening to you, ask your customers to add you to their safe list and explore using alternative words that can mean the same thing as 'free'.

Structuring your newsletter

Think carefully about how you structure your e-mail newsletter. Your structure will encourage people to either read it or to press the delete button instead. Here are four things to consider.

- **The e-mail browse window.** Most people have a browse window open under their e-mail list where they can view the first few lines of what you are saying to them. Capturing their interest from this should be one of your aims.

- **The title of your newsletter.** Some people may decide whether to read your e-mail or to discard it, based on the title of your newsletter. Call it something they don't like and ping, you're in the recycle folder. Possibly a worse place still than the junk folder. Think carefully about the title that will encourage them to open it. Vary this to see what works best. Think about what makes you open or delete a newsletter and ask your friends and colleagues too.

- **Content.** If your newsletter is trying to sell something and nothing more, the chances are it will end up in the recycle bin. As outlined earlier, if you are offering something of value, such as top tips or an interesting case study you may entice the recipient to read beyond the first few lines. Even if your objective is to boost sales, always focus on giving something extra. Make it interesting enough for people to look at so they want to click through to your website. You are reminding customers why they chose to buy from you or signed up to your newsletter and you're letting prospects know why they should be thinking about using you. It's a fact that the Internet is still largely used as a source of information. Having information on your website is important and if you can guide the recipients to your website from your newsletter, you are generating positive traffic. Here are some successful approaches that I have taken.

  o Photographs- my website lends itself to having lots of stunning visuals as it is based on walking and travelling to beautiful places.

  o Competitions -another effective way to get people to click through from my newsletter to my website is to ask a question and offer a prize for the correct answer. If you have a new product for example and you want people to look more closely at it, ask a question about it and give the participants the opportunity to win it. This works wonders. You can use this approach whether you have a physical product to sell as in my case, or you are promoting a service.

  o Graphics versus text content. Many people now have their e-mails set to only receive text-based messages because much of the Spam that is sent comes through

227

in graphics and code called HTML. If you have a newsletter that can only be sent in HTML (code that adds in graphics, links, changes the font etc.) then you could be missing out on communicating with everyone on your list. I send my newsletters in both versions. With the right software, the programme should manage what the recipient receives based on their e-mail setting.

Statistics

As with all of your marketing activities, planning is important, but so is learning what works through a process of trial and error. Don't be afraid to send out different styles of newsletters to see what results you get, but always remember your objectives and why you are sending these newsletters out in the first place. Results are important. They enable you to plan your future e-mail newsletter campaigns in a more targeted way. To do this you have to know who does what with your newsletter. Before you sign up to a software package, look at the statistics it will give you. Statistics that are useful to know include:

- o How many people received the e-mail
- o How many people opened the e-mail
- o Who clicked on what link
- o Who forwarded it to someone else

Good e-mail newsletter software should allow you to record the statistics from any newsletters you send. This will allow you to segment your e-mail list by using different questions and seeing what links the recipients click on. You will also see what products and services generate the most interest, again by seeing what is clicked on. By showing who has opened your newsletter, you can stop mailing those people who automatically delete it every time.

Good software will also manage your client list so that when you get bounce backs (When the e-mail address doesn't exist) you can delete these from your list.

So, e-mail newsletters are a great way of reinforcing what you do and once you have got into the swing of creating them and sending them out, you will wonder what was holding you back. But to start with, explore the software that is out there and if you feel you need a little extra guidance, ask your colleagues and your networking peers how they send out their e-mail newsletters. If in doubt, fall back on your web developer and ask for some help to get you started.

Search Engines

There are currently three main search engines on the Internet - Google, MSN and Yahoo! Around 80% of the searches in the UK are carried out on Google. This goes to show that whatever work you do with regards to your e-marketing, it is always worth ensuring it is compatible with Google. However, who knows, in the future one of the other search engines could well take the lead as the most popular.

At a basic level, search engines send spiders or robots out on a mission through the World Wide Web, looking at billions of pages, indexing and then saving them onto computers, ready to bring up the information that has been searched for in less than a second. It's rather amazing isn't it?

There are many tools that Google will let you use in your e-marketing, completely free of charge. So, if you haven't got an account set up in Google, go to *www.google.co.uk* and register now. Here are a few great tools to get you started:

- **Google Analytics**. This enables you to find out how many people have looked at your website, what part of the world they are from, what links they clicked on and much more. You may need to get your web developer to add Google Analytics to your website.

- **Google Alerts**. You can set up Google Alerts to inform you when a search is made using certain keywords. This is a really useful tool that helps you to see how many searches are being made on a keyword. I use this for developing new product ranges. I will put some product keywords on alert and see how many searches are made for those keywords. If there are many, and I'm confident that I can be competitive with other websites that sell those products, I will consider adding them to my website. Let's now take a different example of say a Mortgage Adviser, working in Horsham that is considering expanding their service to include pensions. It's likely they will want to see how many searches are being made for 'pensions advice,' 'pension information'; 'pension adviser Horsham', 'IFA Horsham' etc. Google Alerts can help by evaluating just how popular search terms are.

- **Blogger**. So you can start writing a blog. More on this later.

- **AdWords**. Paid advertising, based on a pay per click basis. More on this later.

- **Google Maps**. If you put your business on Google's map, potential customers can find you if they search on a locality. This has actually brought new customers straight to my door!

Along with the other search engines, Google will give you many pages of information to read, covering what they look for, how they list pages and many other things that will give invaluable insights into how to do your search engine optimisation so that you can improve your position within the search results. Search engine optimisation is a fascinating subject, one that is always changing as the search engines strive to make their listings the most appropriate to what you are searching for. You can keep in touch with what is happening and get some great tips from many of the SEO forums and websites dedicated to SEO. Try *www.searchenginewatch.com* if you want to access some really useful information and tips on how to get good listings with the search engines.

Google Page Rank

Google Page Rank was devised by the developers of Google to give an idea of the value of importance that Google gives to a page on your website. This is given on a basic scale of 1 to 10. Quite simply the higher the value, the more important Google thinks the page is. Google Page Rank is a very useful tool to find the pages that you want to get links from. Ideally, the higher the rank of the page that links to you, the better.

- **An example of this is the BBC website** with a Google page rank of 9, (On the home page). This means that Google rate the BBC website as important and in the (unlikely!) event that the BBC were to link to your website, then Google will think that your website is also relatively important too, because this prestigious link is classed as a vote for you. This would help to boost your page rank and ratings in the search engines.

- **My links page is rated at 4/10,** which means that Google have rated it quite highly, therefore a link from my links page to another website, will be looked upon more favourably by Google than a link from a page with a rating of say 3/10.

- **My home page has a page rank of 5/10**, (Something I am quite proud of getting and which is possibly based on my web developer giving me a link from one of their 6/10 ranked pages). Have a chat with your web developer and ask if they can do this for you.

How can you find out more about Google Page Rank?

Download the Google toolbar. Go to *www.google.com* and search on 'Google toolbar', then follow the instructions and you will be able to download it. Switch on the Page Rank function. This will send information on what pages you are looking at to Google, so there are some security issues to be aware of. The information that the toolbar sends to Google helps in calculating the rank of a page. This is because the number of times that a web page is looked at helps in the equations that Google use to rank it. If more people are looking at your web pages this will help Google rank your pages as more important.

So, when you embark on optimising your website through the search engines, download the Google toolbar. Look at the rank of the pages that are linking to you and the pages that you want to link to you. Always try and get links from a page with a higher rank than yours.

Search Engine Optimisation (SEO)

SEO is a technical way of saying, "Make your website more visible to search engines like Google and Yahoo! and try to get a good placement in the results page from a search query." There are many people who are experts in this area and you will be inundated (If you haven't already been) with businesses offering to optimise your website. Some will guarantee to get you to the top of a search query's results. It is virtually impossible to guarantee a top placement in the listings from a search query, so be wary of people offering this. If you are tempted, check out their credentials and speak to some of their existing customers before signing up to anything. Before thinking about parting with any money, try out the tips in this section.

The technical people at Google and other search engines are always looking at ways of making the searches more relevant to the searcher and how they do this is a closely guarded secret. Don't despair though. There are still many things that you can do to achieve SEO on a shoestring that will help you get up the listings on the search results organically. This basically means you haven't paid the search engine for a listing, something we look at later in the chapter. Here are three things that can help with your search engine optimisation:

- o Keywords
- o Meta tags and title tags (Meta data fields)
- o Stickiness and website content

We will look at these one at a time, although when you are optimising your website, you need to consider all of them. If you're keen to progress but you still have questions, yes, we've said it before, talk to your web developer!

Keywords

Keywords are a very important part of your website and will in theory, pop up all over it. You will have keywords in your content, they will be built into the code of your website and you will also use them in various fields that the search engines look at and when you want to get a link to your website. It is important to spend time doing your research in this area. Why? Because of what a keyword is.

What is a keyword?

A keyword, or as it's increasingly described, a key phrase, is the term that your potential customer will be searching on to find a product, a service or some other information. Use keywords properly and they can really help with your organic search engine listings. We'll talk later in the chapter about where you need to put them and the best way of using them. But first of all, you need to start with some keyword lists. There are several ways you can do this.

Developing your keywords.

There are some great keyword tools on the Web. These tools will suggest other keywords that people are using as a search query, that relate to the words you are thinking of using. You can get quite technical with this and start looking at keyword analysis, where you can get information on how many searches are made on a keyword, compared to how many websites there are with that keyword (or phrase). The lower the number of websites using your keyword, the lower the competition there is for that keyword, which could in theory help you get higher up in the search query results. However, there may not be that many people searching on it, so the value to you is limited.

How can you find out what keywords you need to use?

Draw up a list of the keywords that you think relate to your website. For example with my website, because I sell equipment for travellers, I would start with keywords such as: sleeping bags, tents, rucksacks and then develop my list from there. Once you have your list, look at Google and Yahoo! These websites are a good place to start because as we mentioned previously, most Internet searches are carried out here.

Google have a keyword selection tool that is free. Although this keyword selection tool is primarily aimed at people wanting to get the best return on investment from paid advertising on Google (By helping them to identify the relevant keywords that people are clicking on), you can still use this tool - even if you have no intention of signing up to paid advertising. These are the reasons why you should look at Google:

- o The Google keyword suggestion tool will give you a list of options for alternative keywords.

- o This list of keywords will also tell you the number of times that a keyword or key phrase was searched on in the last month.

- o It will also tell you the average for the number of searches per month, in the last 12 months.

- o The other valuable addition to this tool is that it will advise you of how competitive a keyword or phrase is. If there are many people competing on that phrase then Google will tell you, using a little bar chart, how competitive that keyword is.

To use this tool you need to go to the Google search page and search on 'Google keyword suggestion' and in the results you will find the link to the tool: https://adwords.google.com/select/KeywordToolExternal. Go to the web page and look at what other keywords you should be using. The good news is that it is pretty simple to use.

Yahoo! have a similar service and offer suggestions for keywords and phrases when you sign up to their paid advertising programme.

As you can imagine, there are many keyword suggestion tools available to you. For example, if you search on the phrase in Google, you will get a return of around 2.2 million pages. Where do you begin?

Wordtracker

I use Wordtracker, (*www.wordtracker.com*) because it enables you to do trial runs of your keywords. (Websites such as Wordtracker get their data from the big search engines) You can sign up for a 7 day free trial so if you are looking for some keywords to get your website more optimised, then this is ideal. Wordtracker also has a huge amount of information that will help you use your keywords effectively. If you decide to subscribe after the free trial there is a price to pay so check out their website for the details. It may be a good investment if you use your keywords actively and are regularly updating them. However, if you're not then it's an expense you're unlikely to get a return on. I found it invaluable when I set up my website.

So, keywords or key phrases are very important to know. You will use them in many places in your website, from the fields that search engines look at, to your website content, back links and paid for advertising on the search engines. (All looked at in this chapter). Spend time researching your keywords and don't assume that people will search for your services or products using the same phrases and words as you. One person's bathroom basin is another person's bathroom sink. Make sure that you find out what keywords are the most popular when people are searching for your products or services.

In summary

- o Thoroughly research the keywords that you want your website to be found on.
- o Use the free tools on Google and Yahoo! in addition to the free trials you can get on other keyword suggestion websites.
- o Think laterally - people searching on the Internet can use the most bizarre terms.

Meta tags and title tags (Meta data fields)

If you find some of the information in this section a little technical, don't worry. Get the general gist of what I'm sharing and then talk to your Web developer if you want to progress this area of SEO further.

First things first, what are meta data fields? They are at the back end of your website. Generally you won't actually see them on your website because they are used to tell the search engines what your website is all about.

There are two main meta data fields that you should know about. These can help your e-marketing and your search engine listings.

- o Meta title fields
- o Meta description fields

What are meta titles?

This is usually the blue bar at the top of the screen that tells you what web page you are on. It is also one of the first things a search engine will look at to see what the web page is all about. Ideally the description should relate to the page. Let me illustrate this by way of example.

I sell a sleeping bag called a 'Rab Quantum 800'. In the title field I have the words, Rab Quantum 800 Sleeping Bag. If you put this search term into the Google search field you will see that this page is at the top of the search listings. Click on the page and you will see the title bar at the top, which has my keywords for that page in it. The keywords are 'Rab Quantum 800 Lightweight Down Sleeping Bag'.

Depending on what you can edit in your website you may be able to put your keywords in this field. If you are not able to do this, then your web developer will be the person responsible. There are two other things I would like to share with you about meta title fields:

o   When you add a page in your favourites, the default name given to the page is the name in the meta title field.

o   The text you use in the meta title field will also be the text that the search engines use in the title of your listings in the search results. If this relates to what the person is searching for they will see your listing much more quickly.

What are meta descriptions?

Again, you won't see the information that is in this field on your web page. Like the meta titles, the search engines use meta descriptions. They are very important because the text in this field is what some search engines will use to describe your page in the search results.

If you can edit the meta description, make sure that you use a description that accurately describes the web page and that contains some of your keywords. This description of your web page is very important as it will help in getting people to click through to your website. You may want to include some of the benefits of why they should click on this link to your website. You can have about 260 characters in this field and Google will generally display around 150 of these characters in their page description.

In summary, meta data fields are important in e-marketing.

- o They tell the search engines what the web page is about
- o The search engines will use the information in their result listings
- o The information can help get people clicking through to your website
- o The information gives a good description of a saved page
- o You can communicate the benefits and give a call to action in the description field

On my website I have control over these fields from the catalogue database. When I add a new product after doing my basic keyword research I complete the title and description fields for each product. This makes the title and description different and relevant for each product so the search engines can return appropriate results to the searcher. The meta data fields are not always editable by the person who owns the website. Your web developer will tell you what you can and can't do.

Your website content and stickiness

Content is king. The Internet was designed to share information and it is still widely used for this purpose. Most SEO experts will agree that the more content you have on your website the better it is for attracting visitors. Before you start to look at the content of your website, you need to find out whether you can add content yourself, using a content management system (CMS), or whether your web developer is the only person that can do this. Ideally, you want to be able to manage the content of your website so that you can keep it fresh with regular updates and changes. Most content management systems are easy to use and it usually takes no more than a few minutes for you to add a piece of news or to change the text on any of your pages. You may even be able to add new pages and keywords to your website with a decent content management system.

Stickiness is the term that is used to describe how long someone stays on your website. Make it sticky and they will stay around longer, whether that means they stay around longer on this visit or they come back hungry, wanting more. Having relevant, engaging and up-to-date content on your website is one of the most effective ways to make your website sticky. I make my website sticky by adding new products, including new travel and gear reviews and adding new photographs of my travels and my customers' travels and walks. Because I am continually updating my website with new content, I have built up a loyal group of repeat visitors. You need to think about how you can make your website sticky. Here are a few ideas for starters:

- **Build up a community around your website.**

- **Use a blog on your website.** If you don't have one built into your website, then link an external one to it. Make sure you keep the blog updated! More on this later.

- **Set up forums on your website.** These are great places where customers and other information seekers can ask questions and share knowledge. They are really useful for encouraging repeat visits.

So how can you generate content on your website?

Think about your target audience. What do they want to know when they come onto your website? At my website, (*www.walkandtravel.com*) I appeal to people who are planning a travel adventure, or they want to go walking. The more information I can include on these topics, with regular updates, the better. This all helps create stickiness. Some of my website content includes:

- o Beginner's guides
- o How to guides
- o Gear reviews
- o Travel reviews
- o Travel tips and advice
- o Travel photos

This really helps attract people who are doing walking and travelling related searches and finding *www.walkandtravel.com* through the search engines. The more people looking at your website the better your rank is in the search engine listings.

Your website is likely to be related to something you are passionate about, which is your business. You will need to find a balance between selling your products and services and actually sharing useful information and knowledge that visitors will welcome and appreciate.

Here are some tips for your website content:

- o Add your newsletter
- o Give your website users some great tips
- o Add testimonials from your customers. Try and include some keywords from your earlier research
- o Ask your customers or suppliers for interesting and appropriate content
- o Write articles using your expertise and knowledge

By regularly adding new content to your website, and updating the existing content, your efforts will pay off in the long run. Visitors will return, knowing that in all probability every time, there's something new and interesting to read or download. It's also worth bearing in mind that search engines love fresh content which is another good reason for updating your website content regularly.

Links

Links are where other websites add the name of your website in their pages and when someone clicks on this link they will be directed to your website. Links will also appear in your website to direct people around your content. Links may also be referred to as hyperlinks. Using links should form an important part of your SEO campaign.

Why are links important?

Links are important to the search engines who follow them to find and index your website and your content. This happens in a split second, as there are millions of websites to get around. As mentioned earlier, the search engines do this using 'robots' and 'spiders' (Not real ones!) but software based on vast racks of computers that access websites and take information from web pages and store them, ready to be accessed as soon as someone runs a search. If they search on your keywords you will pop up in that search, somewhere in the millions of pages that the search engine has stored away.

There are four different types of links.

- **Internal.** These links are internal on your website and therefore important for the spiders to find their way around and index as many pages as they can. They can be the buttons or the text that users click on to take them to other parts of your website. An important technique to get internal links to all your pages is by developing a map of your website. This is known as a sitemap and is basically a page with an internal link from your front page. This page then lists all the pages in your website with an internal link to each one. There are software programmes that can build you a sitemap. Google has one, but in the first instance, I recommend that you talk to your web developer.

- **Two way links.** Two way links are where another website links to your website (external link) and you link back to theirs. These are usually based on reciprocal agreements. External links, (both two way and one way) may also be called back links or anchor text links.

- **One-way link.** A one way link is where another website links to your website, but you don't return the favour by linking to their website. The search engines will actually give your website a better rating if you have a one way link because if someone has put a link to your website it is because it is worthy of a link rather than because you are both doing each other a favour. The more worthy the website is that links to you, the better a search engine will rank it. For example as we mentioned earlier if the BBC links to you, the search engines will give that link real weight and this will help boost your website in the search listings. I'm still striving for a link from the BBC!

- **The anchor text back link.** This is where you get another website to link to you using some of your keywords. This can be done by adding some of your keywords into a link that takes a person to a specific page on your website. You can see now how important these keywords are becoming can't you? When I get back links, I try to base some of them on keywords and then get that keyword, such as 'sleeping bag,' to link directly to my page with sleeping bags on. There is a great case study showing the power of anchor text back links. To find out more look up the words 'miserable failure' on Google. It's an interesting story! Since then, Google have adjusted the way they rank and index pages, looking at many more aspects of web content now.

How do you get links to your website?

There are many ways that you can get links to your website, and it can take some time. There are companies that offer this service, but working on a links strategy is something you can usually consider yourself. At least give it a try! The more quality and relevant back links you have, the more important the search engines will think your website is. Here are some ideas for generating back links:

- o Do your research. Find out the websites that you would like to link to yours and ask if they want to swap links with your website.

o Write articles and add in links to your website, more later!

o Write a blog and add in links to your website.

o Use directory sites. Again, looked at later…

o Ask your web developer if they will case study you and link back to your website.

o Talk to business associates about reciprocal links.

o Ask your suppliers to add links on their website.

o Ask any trade associations you are a member of if they will add your business details plus a link on their website to your website.

In an ideal world we would all have one-way links from relevant websites. Relevancy is something that Google rates highly. For example if you are a mortgage broker, then relevant links would be from estate agents, insurance brokers, mortgage providers and independent financial advisers. You may want to use your keywords to develop anchor text back links. Having good quality and relevant links is something you should aim for.

Who's linking to you?

If you want to find out who is linking to your website, use 'link:' in the search term when you put it in the search box on a search engine followed by your website address. For example I can find out who links to my website by using the search term "link:www.walkandtravel.com". You can also find out the websites that link to your website, by using *www.wholinkstome.com*. This is a great website that gives plenty of link information. If you put your home page web address in speech marks when you search this will show all the websites with exactly the same text. This may also help to identify websites with links to yours. It's an enjoyable exercise finding out how many links you have.

So, if you have no links to your website or just a few, you need to get cracking!

Directories

There are literally thousands of directories on the Web and you could spend your life working through them to get your website listed. Directories range from the well-known ones such as *www. yell.com* to the smaller local directories. For example, your local parish council may well have a website with a small directory of local businesses.

Two of the main directories you should consider trying to get a listing in are:

- **Yahoo!** After spending many hours searching around forums and reading articles, it became apparent to me that you shouldn't really be paying for a directory listing. With one exception that is, the Yahoo! Directory, *http://dir. yahoo.com.* The reason for this is that many of the search engines get their data from the Yahoo! Directory. This will help you get into their listings and, because the directory is from Yahoo! it carries weight as a back link.

- *www.Dmoz.org* is another directory worth trying to get into because it is a directory edited by people that are looking at every website submitted to ensure it is worthy of listing. This can take a while or it can happen quite quickly (I am still waiting!) Because people edit Dmoz, the search engines give this added weight. They use the data in Dmoz to help populate their search listings. Google has a very close relationship with Dmoz.

Although you will find other directories on the Web that are worth considering, make sure that you plan your time carefully. Remember that although any back link is good, a back link from a page that has a higher Google page rank to you is better. When you are researching directories, search on your products and services so that you can see which directories come up in the results. These are most likely the ones to focus your initial efforts on. If you can find a directory that specialises in your field, then the search engines will rate this as a better link, due to the relevancy of the content as mentioned previously. For example a small-business owner I know has a website selling hair accessories. Her website is listed in hundreds of directories, using keywords to anchor her link. This helped get her website to the top of the search listings on her keywords.

If you want to use your website to target local customers then local directories can be useful. A good example of a really effective local directory is 'The Best Of' franchise, *www.thebestof.co.uk* where although you pay to advertise, you benefit from the fact that they can get your business to the top of the search engine listings. As with any paid advertising it is important that you look at how much business you need from your investment. Revisit Chapter 5 if you need to freshen up!

To summarise, with directories:

o   Don't pay to be listed, with the exception of Yahoo! that is unless you are confident of a return on your investment.
o   Try and get a listing on Dmoz

o Try and get keywords in an anchor text back link from the directory.

o If you market your business to local customers, find out about local directories and what they are offering.

o Look out for directories that are relevant to the products or services that you are promoting on your website.

Forums

Dee has covered a fair bit of ground on this particular subject in Chapter 2, so I won't dwell on it too much. Forums are simply websites where people get together to discuss subjects and topics that they share a common interest in. If you find the right forum, you can end up being regarded as a helpful expert, which will boost your online profile. If you try and sell however, you may well be kicked off. Forums are searched on by the search engines so, if you are an active forum participant and you do an online search of your name don't be surprised to see some of the information you have contributed in forums appearing. Identify one or two forums as part of your overall e-marketing strategy, and then join in the discussions.

Articles

Writing and publishing articles online is another great way to build your reputation as an expert in your field. In Chapter 7, there are many tips on how to get press releases and articles published in printed publications that you can also apply to your online articles. There are many article-based websites where you can publish your work. Generally speaking, they will ask for your permission to reproduce any article you have written on other websites. You should always be given the credit for writing the article and hopefully a link back to you and your website. We talked earlier about generating content for your website, well now you are generating content for other people's websites, as an expert in your field. When you are writing any articles and publishing online, you also need to think about adding in your keywords and getting some anchor links back to your website. Some article websites will allow this.

I have personally written articles and published them on Article Alley and A1 Articles. These articles have also been picked up by websites including other articles websites. Being a curious type of person, I search on the keywords or titles of my articles to see where they have been used. You get a warm feeling when you realise that your articles have found their way onto other websites. But make sure that you are given the credit when this happens. To find out more on article websites, search on 'article websites' and thousands will appear. Again focus on the ones that will be of the greatest benefit to your business and find out the reputation of each website before investing time and energy writing articles for them.

The following websites should give you a starting point with your research because they allow articles to be published.

- Article Alley – *www.articlealley.com*
- A1 Articles – *www.a1articles.com*
- Ezinearticles – *www.ezinearticles.com*
- Article City – *www.articlecity.com*
- Articledashboard – *www.articledashboard.com*

Ultimately it comes down to choosing the websites you like the look and feel of and where you can see a clear benefit and value in having your work published.

Web2

Web2 is the phrase that has been coined for the interactive web where you are part of a community or you build your own community. Forums are a simple version of this, but it also widens out to include blogs such as Blogger, and social networking websites such as Facebook, My Space and You Tube to name but a few. There are many other social networking websites. Again, do your research to find out the ones most appropriate to you. Here are three websites I use that have not been discussed so far.

- **MySpace,** (*www.myspace.com*) is used by millions of people across the globe. Many people use this website as a way of keeping in touch with their friends or their community. I don't use it for this, preferring instead to upload content from my website. Search engines have trawled My Space profiles for a number of years now.

- **Blogger**, (*www.blogger.com*) is part of the Google group. It's a place where you can put down your thoughts and ideas. Some people use it as a journal or a diary; others use it as a place to share information. These blogs are then searched and indexed; giving people the information they are looking for. People also go to the website and search Blogger for information on what is happening. With your blog you can up load pictures, add in text, add in back links and generally show that you are an expert or commentator in your field. For example in the outdoors industry, as new products are brought to the market, I am able to share what I think about them on my blog. One small business owner, Becci Coombes, has a website, *www.girlstravelclub.co.uk* that dispenses useful travel advice to women in addition to selling travel related products. Becci is an active blogger and because of this has ended up on the television and in many glossy travel magazines. So, get blogging! You never know, you may be the next business person to appear on television talking about your business!

- **Facebook,** (*www.facebook.com*) is a phenomenon in social networking with thousands of people signing up to it every day and over 110 million active users worldwide. On Facebook you can set up groups and many businesses are using this facility as a promotional tool. In some web forums you may hear rumours that Facebook are planning on shutting these types of groups down. You can invite people to join these groups, and then send messages to everyone in the group, by posting items on the 'wall'. This is an area where you can add text, images and links for everyone to see. You can communicate with your group on Facebook and tell them about the exciting new happenings on your website and with your business. Again, check it out. It may be that you simply use Facebook to keep in touch with your friends because the types of customers you are looking to attract are not to be found on Facebook. On the other hand, you could find yourself in the opposite situation. It comes back to knowing the types of customers that you want to target and then identifying where you can find them.

There are websites that specialise in certain business sectors, with one good example being *www.linkedin.com* a website aimed at business people offering professional services. You can use LinkedIn to upload your professional profile. Because it serves as a virtual electronic networking site, you can invite your contacts to join you, you can link up with other professionals and search for specific business people. LinkedIn is also covered in Chapter 2.

Pay Per Click Advertising

Pay per click advertising, sometimes known as AdWords (which is the name Google have given their pay per click advertising programme), sometimes known as sponsored listings, is where you buy traffic to your website, from a search engine. Google, Yahoo!, MSN and Ask each have their own pay per click programmes that you can work with.

Pay per click adverts are usually located in the column that appears on the right hand side of the search results page. They may also be at the very top of the page in a shaded box, but they are always clearly marked as paid adverts. The concept is very simple. If a person searches on your keywords, your advert will be displayed. If they click on your advert, you will pay for that click. Hence the term 'pay per click'. You set a maximum amount that you are willing to pay for a click and also a maximum daily budget. Once you have spent your daily budget, your advert no longer appears even though people are continuing to search using your keywords. This is very useful for controlling the amount you spend on online advertising. If you are thinking about advertising online in this manner, the same principles apply as for advertising in printed publications. You need to define why you are looking to advertise and whom you are aiming your adverts at. The advice in Chapter 5 is also relevant to your online advertising.

So why consider pay per click advertising?

o It can be an effective way to drive targeted traffic to a new website. You may want people visiting your website before you can get good listings in the free search listings.

o You may have an existing website and you simply want to drive more targeted traffic to it because you are not getting enough traffic from your offline marketing and from your natural SEO.

o   You may want to promote a specific product or service and drive online traffic actively looking for this product or service to your website.

o   You may want to get a large number of people signing up to your e-mail newsletter. Capturing their valuable data will enable you to build targeted e-mail lists.

o   You can control when your adverts are displayed.

o   Your adverts can be written so they match what people are looking for.

How can you set up your pay per click advertising?

Before you actually set up your pay per click advertising, you need to decide on the search engine you are going to use. We have used the example of Google here because most of the searches that are performed in the UK are with Google.

You will need to set up an account with Google, via their home page, *www.google.com* where you then go to the AdWords pages and follow the instructions. It can be fairly straightforward to set up but, you can become very involved with the system, as there are many features that when taken advantage of can help make your campaigns more successful. Here are four important areas to consider with your AdWords campaign:

•   **Keywords**. We looked at keywords earlier in the chapter and explored their importance. They are very important in your pay per click advertising. When you set your campaign up, you will select the keywords and phrases that, when someone searches on them will display your advert. You will also be offered other suggestions for keywords that you may want to include in your campaign. You need to have around 10 keywords for each advert. If you have any more you may find it hard to manage your campaign and you may not get the targeted traffic to your website that you are looking for. Keywords can be added in various forms, for example in a negative way so that if someone searches on that particular term, your advert will not be displayed. They can be displayed using speech marks so that your advert will only be shown when someone searches on that keyword. The last thing that you want is to have your budget drained by people clicking onto your advert even though they have no interest in what you are offering.

- **Advert Text**. This is the text that tells the person what you are offering that will persuade them to click through to your website. You only have a limited number of characters in which to communicate to them. The title of the advert allows you 25 characters including spaces. Try and relate your text to the keywords that the advert relates to. You then have two more lines to persuade the person to click through to your website. These two lines have 35 characters each. I find that for my particular business, adding text such as, 'free delivery' and 'in stock' can lead to higher click through rates. Keep your text simple and focus on features and benefits.

- **Click through rates**. Google will give you really useful statistics that show how well your campaign is working. Click through rates will show as a percentage, how many people click on your advert compared with the amount of times that your advert is shown. If you have a low click through rate you may need to change your text.

- **Tracking your clicks**. It is important to track what happens to the clicks on your adverts so you can see what clicks actually convert to sales. This is vital in helping you to analyse your return on investment. You can buy tools that track this. Google has its own tools via Google Analytics. Because you will need to add code into your website it is likely that you will need to speak to your web developer.

As with all your e-marketing activities, you need to spend time managing your Google AdWords and analysing your results. Pay per click advertising is of vital importance to the search engines because of the huge amounts of revenue it generates. If you are seriously considering spending a big portion of your marketing budget on this, it could be worth your while using the services of a Google AdWords Qualified Professional, or at least getting some training.

To conclude

E-marketing is a huge subject and although we have only scratched the surface here, I hope that you feel more confident that with a little research and practice, you can begin to make some positive changes without spending a huge sum of money. Good luck.

Useful Resources

In some chapters I have recommended that you consider using the services of other professionals to help you progress your marketing. Sometimes it can be challenging knowing the right people to speak to. Here are the details of six very good small businesses that I recommend wholeheartedly. As a starting point, you may want to contact them for an informal chat.

AGP Grafico
Pop-up banners, exhibition stands, signs and vehicle graphics.
Contact: Greg Davies
www.agp-grafico.co.uk

Click Up
Google Adwords qualified professional providing individual and group training workshops, full management and consultancy service.
Contact: Steve Cambridge
www.ClickUp.co.uk

Creative Vision Promotions
Promotional gifts and corporate clothing.
Contact: Paul Sheldrake
www.creativevisionpromotions.co.uk

Local Web Solutions/LWS Creative
Websites, blogs, search engine optimisation, design and print.
Contact: Claire Love-Jones
www.lws-uk.com

Profitable Websites
Websites, databases, forums and chat rooms, search engine optimisation.
Contact: Grant Moyse
www.profitablewebsites.co.uk

Speak with Confidence
Public speaking coaching on a one-to-one basis and delegate based workshops.
Contact: Meg Heyworth
www.speak-with-confidence.co.uk

To Order Further Copies

If you would like to purchase any further copies of this book,
you can order and pay online at:

www.themarketinggym.org